Travel Guide To Oman 2023

Discover the Hidden Gems of Oman: A Comprehensive Travel Guide for 2023

Scott O. Cortes

Table of Contents

INTRODUCTION

Welcome to Oman

Welcome to Oman, a country with enthralling natural beauty and a rich cultural history. Oman, a country located on the Arabian Peninsula's southeast coast, entices visitors with its immaculate beaches, stunning mountains, and vast deserts.

Oman has everything you're looking for, whether you're looking for adventure, relaxation, or an immersion into a rich history and culture.

This thorough travel guide is intended to be your go-to travel companion as you set off on your trip across Oman in 2023. It has been painstakingly designed to give you important details, insider knowledge, and undiscovered treasures that will improve your experience and enable you to get the most out of your trip.

The key attractions in Oman, including the vibrant capital city of Muscat as well as the peaceful beach towns, rough mountains, and spectacular natural wonders, are described in detail on the following pages. Engage with the friendly and welcoming Omani people while experiencing Oman's diverse culture and unique cuisine.

This book will help you with every element of your trip, whether you're planning a solo adventure, a family holiday, or a romantic break. We have you covered with all you need to know, including useful suggestions on visa requirements, health and safety precautions, and the ideal times to travel.

Discover Muscat's mysteries, stroll along exquisite beaches, go on a desert safari, tour historic forts and UNESCO World Heritage Sites, and engage in exhilarating outdoor pursuits. Explore Oman's hidden gems, take in its breathtaking scenery, and make lifelong memories.

Prepare to go out on a memorable vacation as we bring to you "Travel Guide to Oman 2023: Discover the Hidden Gems of Oman." The journey has begun!

About This Guide

The "Travel Guide to Oman 2023: Discover the Hidden Gems of Oman" is a thorough and current guide created to give you all the information and insights you'll need for an unforgettable trip to Oman in 2023. This guide is intended to be your go-to travel companion, regardless of whether you've been to Oman before or not.

What to anticipate from this guide is as follows:

- **In-depth Coverage:** This guide provides comprehensive coverage of Oman's main cities, tourist destinations, and natural wonders, including Muscat, the coast, the mountains, the desert, cultural landmarks, and outdoor activities. You'll find comprehensive details on each place, including the main attractions, must-see locations, and useful advice.

- **Insider Advice:** Explore undiscovered jewels and off-the-beaten-path sites to give your trip to Oman an unique flair. Take advantage of local knowledge and suggestions for lesser-known sights, cuisine, customs, and cultural experiences.

- **Practical Information:** This book offers vital details to help you efficiently organise your trip, from visa requirements and transportation options to health and safety advice. Along with advice on when to go, packing necessities, language and communication, and suggested travel applications, you'll also find information here.

- **Cultural Insights:** Through sections on Omani customs, food, art, and etiquette, you can fully appreciate Oman's rich cultural legacy. Improve your contacts with the Omani people and gain a greater grasp of regional cultures.

- **Outdoor Adventures:** This book emphasises several activities like scuba diving, trekking, rock climbing, and more. Oman is a paradise for outdoor enthusiasts. Find exciting adventures and useful advice for participating in these activities safely.

- **Appendix**: To help you better understand Oman, the guide contains helpful information including Arabic words and emergency contacts.

We hope that this book will become your reliable travel companion, assisting you in discovering Oman's treasures and ensuring a memorable and satisfying trip. Enjoy your trip through Oman, and may it be chock-full of priceless memories and life-changing experiences.

Practical Information

It's crucial to have useful information available when organising your trip to Oman in 2023. The information in this part will help you get ready for your trip and make the most of your time in Oman.

- **Visa Requirements:**Check your home country's criteria for visas. Others may need to apply for a visa in advance, while some nations can enter the country without a visa or with one upon arrival. For the latest information, go to the Royal Oman Police's official website or contact the embassy or consulate of Oman that is closest to you.

- **Ideal Season to Visit:**The desert region of Oman experiences hot summers and mild winters. The greatest time to travel is between November and March, when temperatures are more suitable for sightseeing and outdoor activities.

- **Safety and Health**:To make sure you are up to date on normal immunizations before your trip to

Oman, it is essential to speak with a healthcare provider or travel clinic. Additionally, having travel insurance that includes medical coverage is advised.

- Although Oman is a generally safe country, it is always advisable to exercise common sense care. Respect the traditions and customs of the place, and keep an eye out for your possessions while crowded. Call 9999 for police assistance in an emergency.

- **Money & Currency:**The Omani Rial (OMR) is Oman's legal tender. Most businesses accept credit cards, and ATMs are commonly available in large cities and towns. It's a good idea to have some cash on hand for smaller merchants and outlying locations.

- **Communication through Language:**Although Arabic is the official language, English is commonly used, particularly in hotels and tourist areas. During your travels, communication shouldn't be a huge problem.

- **Transportation:**In order to have flexibility and convenience while experiencing Oman, many people choose to rent a car. Foreign driver's licences are typically accepted. Taxis, buses, and shared minibosses (also known as "baiza" or "coasters") are available as public transit choices.

There are reputable cab services, including ride-hailing applications, in large cities like Muscat.
There are also domestic planes that connect major cities and areas.

- **Accommodation:**Oman has a variety of lodging choices to fit different needs and interests. You can choose from accommodations that suit your preferences, such as five-star resorts and hotels, guesthouses, apartments, and desert camping. It is advised to make reservations for lodging in advance, especially during the busiest travel times.

- **Communication through Language:**Although Arabic is the official language, English is commonly used, particularly in hotels and tourist areas. During your travels, communication shouldn't be a huge problem.

- **Local customs and etiquette**:Oman is a Muslim nation with a vibrant cultural heritage. Respecting regional traditions and dressing modestly is crucial, especially when visiting places of worship. Avoid making public demonstrations of affection, and always get permission before taking pictures of locals, especially women.

- **Advisable travel applications:**To improve your trip experience in Oman, use travel applications with features like maps, language translators, and weather updates. Popular applications include Oman Weather, Omani Translator, and Google Maps.

As you get closer to your travel dates, remember to check for any new travel warnings or particular needs. In 2023, you can travel to Oman easily and enjoyably by being well-informed and organised.

PLANNING YOUR TRIP

Best Time to Visit

The best time to travel to Oman is between November and March, when the weather is cooler and better suitable for sightseeing and outdoor sports. The average temperature during this time is pleasant, averaging between 20°C and 30°C (68°F and 86°F) during the day and cooler at night.

When arranging your trip to Oman, keep the following things in mind:

- Oman experiences hot summers and comparatively cold winters due to its desert climate. The country's varied landscapes may be explored and outdoor activities can be enjoyed more comfortably throughout the winter months.

- Visiting major sights, including Muscat's historical monuments, marvelling at the breathtaking wadis (river valleys), going on a mountain hike, and taking part in beach activities, is made easier during the cooler months.

- **Festivals & Events:** Throughout the winter, Oman hosts a number of cultural and traditional events. Omani culture, art, and entertainment are on display during the Muscat Festival, which takes place in January and February. Another notable event that occurs outside of the regular winter season is the Salalah Tourism Festival, which takes place in July and August.

- **Wildlife & Natural Wonders**: Since migratory birds swarm Oman's wetlands and reserves in the winter, it's a great time to be a wildlife enthusiast. It's also a perfect time to go snorkelling or scuba diving in the coastal areas to learn more about the rich marine life.

- **Crowds and Costs**: In Oman, the wintertime is regarded as the busiest travel period. At major attractions, you can anticipate greater crowds and more expensive hotel and flight rates. To ensure that you have your first choice of accommodations and activities, it is important to make your reservations well in advance.

- Travelling to Oman in the shoulder seasons of November to December and February to March can also be fun if you want to avoid crowds and are okay with warmer weather. These months provide an excellent compromise between pleasant weather and less visitors.

- However, it's necessary to take into account different times of the year if you intend to concentrate on particular activities like turtle hatching or exploring the distinctive monsoon season in the Dhofar region. A rewarding and memorable trip to Oman can be achieved by doing your research and designing your itinerary based on your interests and preferences.

For the most up-to-date information, always check weather predictions and local conditions closer to your travel dates.

Visa Requirements

Depending on your country of origin, Oman requires a different type of visa. An outline of Oman's visa requirements is provided below:

- **Visa-Free Entry**: For a limited time, Oman is open to certain nations' nationals without requiring a visa. These nations include the United States, Canada, the United Kingdom, Australia, New Zealand, and the majority of the European Union member states, with a cutoff date of September 2021, to the best of my knowledge.

  Depending on their nationality, visitors from these nations may enter Oman without a visa for stays of up to 10 days, 30 days, or 90 days. Please be aware that the period of the visa-free stay and eligibility may change, thus it is advised to contact the Omani embassy or consulate in your area for the most recent details.

- **Visa on Arrival:** At Oman airports or land border crossings, citizens of a number of nations may obtain a visa at the time of arrival. This makes it possible for travellers to Oman to obtain a visa upon arrival, usually for a stay of up to 30 days. In most cases, a visa on arrival can be extended for an extra 30 days if necessary. However, depending on your country, it is crucial to confirm the precise requirements and eligibility standards for the visa on arrival option.

- **E-Visa:** Oman also has an electronic visa system that enables visitors from certain nations to apply for a visa online before their arrival. The e-visa can be used for travel, business, or family visits, and is normally given for stays up to 30 days. The required documentation must be submitted, and the online visa price must be paid. The e-visa is sent electronically once it has been accepted, and travellers can print it out and submit it when they arrive in Oman.

- **Prior Visa:** Prior to travelling to Oman, several nations must get a visa from an Omani embassy or consulate. Visitors from nations including India, Pakistan, China, and several African countries are subject to this. If this describes you, you must send the necessary paperwork, which includes a visa application form, passport images, and supporting documents, to the closest Omani diplomatic mission well in advance of the dates of your intended journey.

- For the most precise and recent information regarding visa requirements for your particular nationality, you must check the Royal Oman Police's (ROP) official website or contact the nearby Omani embassy or consulate. They can give you the appropriate advice regarding the application procedure, costs, and any most current adjustments to visa rules.

It's important to keep educated and make sure you have the right visa before flying to Oman because visa laws and criteria can change over time.

Health and Safety Tips

Prioritising your health and safety when visiting Oman is crucial for a hassle-free and pleasurable trip. Here are some crucial health and safety advice to take into account:

- **Travel insurance**: Having travel insurance that pays for medical costs, emergency evacuation, and trip cancellation or interruption is strongly advised. Verify the policy's specifics to be sure it offers sufficient protection for your needs.

- **Preparing medically:**Before departing for Oman, seek advice from a doctor or travel clinic. Based on your medical history and the current state of health in Oman, they can advise you on the appropriate shots and prescriptions.

- Pack a simple first aid pack for travel that contains all the necessities, such as bandages, antiseptic cream, pain relievers, and any required prescription drugs.

- Keep Hydrated: Oman has a desert climate, making it particularly hot throughout the summer. Drink plenty of water to stay hydrated even if you don't feel thirsty. Always keep a refillable water bottle with you.

- **Using Sunscreen**:Put on sunscreen with a high SPF, a hat, sunglasses, and light, breathable clothing that covers your skin to protect yourself from the intense sun.

- During the hottest hours of the day, which are often between 10 am and 4 pm, seek shade.

- **Respect for regional traditions and customs:**Oman is a conservative nation with a rich cultural heritage. Particularly while visiting religious places and dealing with locals, show respect for cultural traditions, dress modestly, and be aware of local sensitivities.

  Avoid showing affection in public as it could be seen as inappropriate.

- **Stay Up to Date:**Keep abreast of any travel warnings or security alerts issued by your government or the local authorities, as well as the current state of affairs in Oman. Sign up for emergency notifications at your embassy or consulate.

- **Driving Safety:**Make sure you are familiar with the local traffic laws and regulations before driving in Oman.

Be extra cautious, especially in rural and highway regions.

- Especially in rural and arid areas, keep an eye out for wandering camels or other animals on the highways.

- **Swimming Safety:**Use caution and adhcrc to safcty proccdures when participating in water-related activities. Only swim in places that are specified, and be aware of strong currents or tides.

- Make sure you are properly trained, are using dependable equipment, and are adhering to all safety recommendations given by qualified operators before you go snorkelling or scuba diving.

- **Protect Your Property:**Take steps to protect your possessions and treasures. When available, use hotel safes or secure lockers, and keep an eye out in crowded places.

- **Emergency numbers:**For quick access, save crucial emergency contact information, such as the phone numbers for your local police department, medical services, and your embassy or consulate, on your phone or on paper.

Before your journey to Oman, it's a good idea to review the most recent health and safety recommendations from reliable sources, such as the World Health Organization (WHO) and the travel advisory websites of your government. You can travel safely and enjoy yourself in Oman by being aware and taking the appropriate safety precautions.

Packing Essentials

It's crucial to pack for your vacation to Oman by taking the climate, customs, and activities you'll be participating in into account. The following is a list of things you must bring:

- Pack breathable, lightweight clothing that is appropriate for warmer temperatures. When visiting holy locations, in particular, dress modestly and loosely. To shield yourself from the sun and insects, think about wearing long sleeves and pants.

- Oman experiences intense sunlight, therefore bring the following necessary sun protection items:
- High SPF sun protection
- Broad-brimmed cap or hat
- Sunglasses that block UV rays

- **Cosy shoes:** Due to the likelihood that you will be exploring a variety of attractions and terrains, wear comfortable walking shoes or sandals. Consider wearing sturdy hiking boots or shoes if you intend to go hiking.

- Pack swimwear if you plan to take advantage of Oman's stunning beaches or engage in water sports.

- When visiting religious places or more conservative areas, women may choose to take a scarf or shawl to cover their heads and shoulders.

- Consider taking a travel adaptor if you plan to charge your electronic gadgets in Oman because of the country's Type G electrical connector.

- **Travel papers:**Make sure your passport is valid for at least six months after the day you plan to depart.

- Make sure you have the proper visa or visa on arrival papers, depending on your nationality.
- Airline tickets: The electronic versions of your tickets can be saved or printed.
- Hotel or other reservations: Save copies of your travel arrangements.

- **Λ first aid kit including medications:**Prescription Drugs: If you are on any prescription drugs, make sure you bring enough of them for the duration of your trip, as well as a copy of your prescription.
- A basic first aid kit should contain the following items: bandages, antiseptic ointment, painkillers, motion sickness medication (if required), and any other personal drugs.

- **Travel necessities:**Keep your valuable travel documents, like passports, visas, and cash, organised and secure in a travel wallet or pouch.

- Carry enough Omani Rials in cash for smaller businesses and outlying locations. In major cities and popular tourist destinations, credit cards are readily accepted.
- Carrying a reusable water bottle and filling it up frequently will help you stay hydrated.
- Use insect repellent to ward off mosquitoes and other pesky insects, especially if you're going camping or to a wadi.
- Travel Towel: When going to the beach or engaging in other water sports, think about bringing a compact, quickly-drying travel towel.
- Keep a portable power bank on hand to recharge your electrical devices while you're on the go.

- **Elective Items**:If you intend to snorkel, think about bringing your mask, snorkel, and fins for a more comfortable and customised experience.

Binoculars can improve your experience if you're interested in spotting wildlife or watching birds.
Keep in mind to pack for the season and the exact activities you intend to do. It's always a good idea to check the weather forecast closer to the time of your trip and modify your packing list as necessary.

Money and Currency

The Omani Rial (OMR) is Oman's legal tender. When travelling to Oman, it's vital to be aware of the following:

- **Number of Baisa in an Omani Rial:** There are 1,000 baisa in an Omani Rial. Coins come in values of 5, 10, 25, 50, and 100 baisa, while banknotes come in denominations of 5, 10, 20, and 50 rials.

- **Exchange Rate:** The value of the Omani Rial is subject to change. Before your journey, it is wise to verify the exchange rate. Airports, banks, and exchange offices all around Oman offer currency exchange services.

- Despite the widespread acceptance of credit cards in bigger venues, it is nevertheless advisable to carry some cash, especially when visiting smaller vendors, neighbourhood markets, or distant locations where card acceptance may be constrained.

- **ATMs:** In Oman's major cities and towns, ATMs are extensively available. They give you a practical way to use your debit or credit card to make cash withdrawals. Make sure your card can handle overseas transactions, and ask your bank if there are any costs or limitations for making international withdrawals.

- **Currency Exchange:** In Oman, currency exchange services are provided by banks and exchange bureaus. In general, banks are open for longer, and certain exchange offices may impose a minor fee for money conversion. To get the greatest deal, it's a good idea to compare exchange rates and costs.

- Before leaving for Oman, let your bank or credit card provider know about your trip plans to prevent any problems with card transactions. If your bank is unaware of your vacation plans, it may flag overseas transactions as potentially fraudulent.

- **Tipping**: Although not required in Oman, good service is appreciated with a tip. In restaurants and for services rendered by hotel personnel or tour guides, it's typical to round up the price or give a little gratuity of around 10%.

- **Traveler's checks:** In Oman, they are typically not frequently recognized. It is advised to use cash or a credit card to cover your expenses.

- **False Currency:** It is best to exchange money at reputed banks or exchange offices to prevent receiving fake money. To confirm the legitimacy of Omani banknotes, become familiar with their security measures.

- Oman does not have any precise limitations on the amount of money visitors may carry into the country. To minimise any potential problems, it is advised to report any considerable amounts of cash when you arrive.

- Use hotel safes or secure pouches to keep your money safe while you're travelling. Additionally, it's a good idea to keep little bills on hand for convenience's sake and to have your bank's emergency contact information on hand in case your cards experience any problems.

You can efficiently control your spending during your trip to Oman by being aware of currency issues and carrying both cash and credit cards.

EXPLORING MUSCAT

Discovering the Capital City

Oman's capital city, Muscat, is a fascinating fusion of its country's past, present, and future. Here are some of Muscat's top sights and attractions to check out:

- Visit the Sultan Qaboos Grand Mosque, one of Muscat's most recognizable landmarks, to begin your trip. Admire the main prayer hall's massive Swarovski crystal chandelier, gorgeous chandeliers, and complex Islamic architecture.

- **Royal Opera House:** Attending a performance at the Royal Opera House will allow you to fully appreciate Muscat's vast cultural diversity. Opera, ballet, and classical music performances are just a few of the top productions held at this architectural marvel.

- **Mutrah Corniche:** Enjoy a stroll along this beautiful coastal promenade in Mutrah. Admire the port, the classic shows (wooden boats), and the bustling Mutrah Souq, where you can buy Omani trinkets, jewellery, and crafts.

- The mediaeval forts Al Jalali and Al Mirani, which overlook the port, are enduring reminders of Muscat's past. They offer a beautiful backdrop for photographs even if they aren't accessible to the general public.

- The formal palace of the Sultan of Oman is located in Muscat and is known as Qasr Al Alam Royal Palace. The palace is closed off, but you can still view it from the outside and take in the splendour of the gardens that surround it.

- Visit the private Bait Al Zubair Museum to fully immerse yourself in Omani culture and history. Explore the displays that feature historical photos, jewellery, clothing, and other typical Omani artefacts.

- Visit the hilltop park Al Riyam Park and Sultan's Armed Forces Museum for sweeping views of the city and the coast. The Sultan's Armed Forces Museum, which houses military items and exhibitions about Oman's military history, is located inside the park.

- Qurum Beach is a well-liked beach in Muscat where you may unwind and relax. Take pleasure in water sports or a relaxing picnic while taking advantage of the fine white beach and tranquil turquoise waters.

- **Omani French Museum:** This delightful museum, set in a gorgeously restored Omani-French colonial mansion, provides information on the historical connections between Oman and France. Investigate the displays that show how the two countries' cultures have interacted.

- **National Museum of Oman**: The National Museum, which is slated to open in 2023, will provide a thorough exploration of Oman's history, heritage, and culture. It will feature a variety of artefacts and engaging exhibits that illustrate the nation's illustrious past.

Enjoy traditional Omani restaurants serving regional food as you tour Muscat, or visit one of the many international eateries to experience flavours from around the world. Muscat's bustling atmosphere ensures a memorable and enriching experience, as do its architectural marvels and cultural riches.

Sultan Qaboos:Grand Mosque

One of Muscat, Oman's most famous landmarks is the Sultan Qaboos Grand Mosque, a work of art in architecture. Here are some details regarding this stunning mosque:

- The mosque's design and architecture are a fusion of Islamic, Omani, and modern elements. It was constructed in the late 20th century. It exhibits deft craftsmanship and close attention to detail. One of the largest hand-woven carpets in the world and a magnificent crystal chandelier may be found in the main prayer hall.

- The mosque is called Sultan Qaboos after the late Sultan of Oman, Qaboos bin Said Al Said. He contributed significantly to Oman's modernization and was well renowned for his work to advance religious tolerance and cultural survival.

- **Prayer Hall**: The mosque's main prayer hall has space for a large number of worshipers. Beautiful Islamic decorations, vivid stained glass windows, and elaborate calligraphy are all featured within. Before entering, visitors must remove their shoes and dress modestly.

- The mosque has a large clock tower that prominently shows the prayer times, including the Azaan (call to prayer), as well as the time. It is a significant landmark in Muscat and is visible from a distance.

- **Gardens and Courtyards**: There are lovely, well-kept gardens and roomy courtyards all around the mosque. These places offer a peaceful atmosphere and are ideal for reflection and relaxation.

- **Non-Muslim Visitors**: The Sultan Qaboos Grand Mosque welcomes non-Muslim guests who can enjoy its magnificent architecture and discover more about Islamic customs. Visitors must observe the mosque's dress code, which calls for modest attire and headscarves for women, to respect the mosque's holiness.

- **Islamic Library**: The mosque is home to a library that has a sizable collection of Islamic literature. These materials are available to academics and researchers who want to learn more about Islam and related topics.

- **Guided Tours**: Visitors can take advantage of guided tours to learn more about the mosque's history, architecture, and spiritual significance. The excursions provide visitors with a fuller appreciation of

Omani culture and the mosque's significance to the neighbourhood.

- The mosque is especially attractive at night when it is exquisitely illuminated, producing a breathtaking spectacle. The mosque's tranquil atmosphere is enhanced by the soft lighting, which highlights the mosque's architectural elements.

Anyone exploring Muscat must go to the Sultan Qaboos Grand Mosque. All visitors will have a wonderful experience at this place because of the alluring combination of architectural beauty, cultural relevance, and spiritual peace it gives.

Royal Opera House Muscat

In Muscat, Oman's capital city, there is a wonderful performing arts centre called the Royal Opera House Muscat. Here are some details regarding this cultural treasure:

- **Architecture and Design:** The Royal Opera House Muscat is a stunning architectural marvel that skillfully combines contemporary aesthetics with traditional Omani design features. The exterior is beautiful, with a front that is artistically ornamented, huge arches, and fine craftsmanship.

- The opera house was established in 2011 to foster and promote the arts and culture in Oman and the surrounding area. It acts as a stage for exhibiting regional artists and hosting concerts from abroad.

- Opera, ballet, classical music concerts, Arabic music, theatre, and dance are just a few of the world-class acts that are presented at the Royal Opera House in Muscat. Its stage is graced by renowned performers and organisations from around the world, offering viewers unparalleled cultural encounters.

- **Opera House Theater:** The opera house's main theatre is built to the greatest acoustic and technical standards. The theatre can accommodate about 1,100 people and offers a cosy atmosphere with good visibility and sound from every seat.

- **Additional Performance Spaces:** In addition to the main theatre, the opera house has a smaller auditorium, a jazz theatre, and an outdoor area for a variety of outdoor activities.

- **Programs for cultural and academic development:** The Royal Opera House Muscat is dedicated to advancing educational and cultural development. It provides a variety of educational programs, workshops, and masterclasses to foster new talent and encourage community involvement.

- Gardens around the opera house, known as the Royal Opera House Gardens, offer a tranquil and attractive ambiance. Visitors can take strolls around the verdant landscape, take in the outdoor atmosphere, and get breathtaking views of the opera theatre.

- **Dining and Amenities:** The opera house complex has several restaurants and cafes where guests can relax before a performance or meet up afterward. Additionally, there is a gift shop where guests can find unusual mementos and cultural objects.

- **Architecture Tours:** The Royal Opera House Muscat offers guided tours that provide visitors with an understanding of the building's architectural significance, the workings of the backstage area, and the rich history that went into its construction. These excursions provide an inside look at the performing arts industry.

- **Accessibility:** The opera house wants to ensure that everyone can see performances. It provides amenities for people with impairments, such as wheelchair access, extra help if needed, and allocated seating.

The Royal Opera House Muscat is evidence of Oman's dedication to the creative industries, cross-cultural dialogue, and aesthetic quality. It offers a compelling setting for outstanding performances and enriching encounters, providing guests with long-lasting memories of Muscat's thriving cultural scene.

Mutrah Souq

In the Mutrah neighbourhood of Muscat, Oman, there is a bustling traditional market called Mutrah Souq. Here are some details regarding this bustling souq:

- Mutrah Souq has a long, illustrious history that goes back several centuries. It served as a crucial trading hub for travellers from Muscat's thriving port.

- An authentic Omani shopping experience may be had at the souq, which displays the nation's rich history, traditional crafts, and cultural treasures.

- **Traditional Buildings:** The souq is located among a maze of winding lanes and traditional buildings with distinctive Omani architectural features, such as lovely wooden doors, carved balconies, and latticed windows.

- **Variety of Products**: Mutrah Souq is well-known for its wide selection of products, which includes traditional Omani handicrafts, jewellery, textiles, spices, fragrances, antiques, mementos, and regional artwork. It's a gold mine for anybody looking for distinctive and genuine Omani goods.

- The market for frankincense, a resinous aromatic substance of special cultural and historical value in Oman, is one of Muttrah Souq's highlights. The variety of frankincense goods available to customers includes resin, oils, incense burners, and perfumes.

- **Haggling and Bargaining:** Visitors to the souq can engage in cordial talks with the vendors to obtain the best pricing. Bargaining is a frequent activity there. It enhances the dynamic environment and gives you a chance to talk to the local store owners.

- **Traditional Souq Experience**: The lively atmosphere, brilliant colours, aromatic spices, and the sounds of haggling and conversation make the souq a sensory joy. It's a terrific location to become fully immersed in the community's culture and experience the authentic Omani atmosphere.

- **Cafés and Restaurants**: There are a number of tiny cafés and restaurants located inside the souq where shoppers can take a break and savour traditional Omani food, snacks, or a cup of Omani coffee.

- **Evening strolls:** As the day cools off and the market is lighted with soothing lighting, Mutrah Souq comes to life. It's the ideal time to take a leisurely stroll, take in the magical atmosphere, and browse the shops more slowly.

- **Corniche proximity**: The Mutrah Corniche, a lovely waterfront promenade, is right next to the souq. By taking a stroll along the corniche, visitors can broaden their investigation while taking in the harbour views and the area's marine culture.

Anyone looking for a distinctive shopping experience and an insight into the lively Omani culture must go to Mutrah Souq. It's a location where old-world craftsmanship, a storied past, and friendly hospitality come together to provide guests an outstanding experience.

Bait Al Zubair Museum

In Muscat, Oman, there is a privately owned museum called the Bait Al Zubair Museum. Here are some details regarding this cultural treasure:

- **Family-Owned Museum:** The Zubair family, who have influenced the preservation of Omani history and the advancement of cultural understanding, founded the Bait Al Zubair Museum.

- **Residence in History:** The museum is set in a magnificently renovated Omani mansion that features conventional Omani architecture and style. It gives tourists a look at the way of life of prosperous Omani families in the past.

- Omani artefacts and exhibits may be found throughout the museum, including traditional clothing, jewellery, weapons, household items, and ancient pictures. These displays offer information about Omani history, culture, and customs.

- **Omani Heritage Gallery:** The Omani Heritage Gallery, which features objects that represent all facets of Omani heritage, including pottery, silverware, textiles, and traditional crafts, is one of the museum's attractions. Visitors can discover more about these artefacts' exceptional craftsmanship and cultural value.

- **Coin Collection:** The Bait Al Zubair Museum has a sizable collection of coins from many eras and civilizations, providing a fascinating look at Oman's history and its connections to other areas through commerce.

- With its courtyards, majlis (sitting spaces), and elaborate décor, the museum's interior is made to look like a traditional Omani home. Visitors can imagine life in an Omani home thanks to this setting's immersive experience.

- **Gift Shop:** The museum contains a gift shop where visitors can buy books, Omani-made crafts, and souvenirs. It's a fantastic location to find one-of-a-kind souvenirs to remember your trip to Oman.

- **Events and Activities of a Cultural Nature:** The Bait Al Zubair Museum frequently conducts cultural gatherings, exhibitions, and educational initiatives that support Omani culture and artistic expression. Opportunities to interact with Omani art, music, and traditional performances are presented by these events.

- **Omani cuisine**: Visitors can enjoy the flavours of Omani cuisine in a charming setting at the museum's on-site restaurant, Bait Al Daleel, which features a delicious array of Omani dishes.

- **Community Engagement:** The Bait Al Zubair Museum collaborates with educational and community outreach programs, as well as institutions of higher learning and cultural institutions. Both locals and foreign tourists are encouraged to become aware of and appreciate Omani heritage.

A journey into Oman's rich cultural heritage is provided by a visit to Bait Al Zubair Museum. It enables guests to learn more about Omani culture while exploring the nation's customs, craftsmanship, and historical legacy.

Qasr Al Alam Royal Palace

The Sultan of Oman's official residence is in Muscat and is called Alam Palace or Qasr Al Alam Royal Palace. Here are some details about this famous palace:

- Qasr Al Alam Palace is renowned for its magnificent architecture and opulence. With its opulent façade, golden accents, and vibrant colours, it exhibits a fusion of modern Islamic and Omani architectural styles.

- The palace is strategically located in the centre of Muscat, overlooking the lovely Muscat Bay, and is bordered by the forts of Al Jalali and Al Mirani. The palace's desirable location enhances its allure and provides breathtaking views of the surroundings.

- **Official Residence**: The Sultan of Oman's ceremonial palace and residence is called Qasr Al Alam. It is used to host official events, host dignitaries, and conduct significant state business.

- **Gardens and Surroundings:** Beautifully maintained gardens surround the palace, adding to its opulence. Lush green lawns, bright flowers, and carefully groomed pathways provide a quiet and inviting ambiance.

- **Changing of the Guards:** Visitors can observe the magnificent Changing of the Guards event that takes place outside the palace. The guards, clothed in their traditional clothing, carry out a beautifully orchestrated march that exhibits Omani military traditions.

- **Photo Opportunities:** While admission into the palace is restricted to authorised employees only, tourists can still get breathtaking photographs of the palace from the exterior. The magnificent building and scenic backdrop give fantastic photo opportunities.

- **Cultural Significance:** Qasr Al Alam Palace is a symbol of Oman's rich history and the country's monarchy. It represents the Sultanate's strong ties to its traditions, heritage, and the ruling Al Said dynasty.

- **Historical Relevance:** The palace was erected in the early 1970s and played a vital part in the modernization and development of Oman under the reign of Sultan Qaboos bin Said Al Said.

- **Accessibility**: While the interior of the palace is not open to the public, visitors can observe the castle's magnificence from outside the gates and enjoy the lovely surroundings.

- **Proximity to Other Attractions:** Qasr Al Alam Palace is located in close proximity to other notable monuments in Muscat, including the Mutrah Corniche, Mutrah Souq, and the Al Jalali and Al Mirani forts. Visitors can explore these attractions in conjunction with a visit to the palace.

- Qasr Al Alam Royal Palace stands as an emblem of Oman's rich heritage and its enduring monarchy. Its architectural splendour and strategic location make it an iconic landmark in Muscat, attracting visitors who appreciate its cultural and historical significance.

Corniche and Mutrah Harbor

The Corniche and Mutrah Harbor in Muscat, Oman, offer a picturesque waterfront area that combines natural beauty with historical significance. Here's some information on these interesting destinations:

- **Scenic Waterfront Promenade**: The Corniche is a stunning waterfront promenade that spans along the coastline of Muscat, affording panoramic views of the Arabian Sea. It's a popular area for locals and tourists to enjoy leisurely walks, jog, or simply rest while taking in the magnificent surroundings.

- **Mutrah seaport:** Mutrah Harbor, located along the Corniche, is a historic and lively seaport that has been a key commercial port for generations. The harbour is recognized for its dynamic ambiance, classic wooden shows (sailing vessels), and fishing boats that dot the seas.

- **Traditional nautical Culture:** Mutrah Harbor provides a look into Oman's rich nautical heritage and fishing customs. Visitors can observe fishermen unloading their catches and repairing their nets, immersing themselves in the real sights and sounds of the local nautical culture.

- **Mutrah Corniche Souq:** Adjacent to the port is the famed Mutrah Souq, a large traditional market where visitors may explore a maze of small lanes filled with booths offering a broad variety of goods. It's a fantastic spot to purchase for traditional Omani handicrafts, textiles, jewellery, spices, and souvenirs.

- **Fish Market**: The Fish Market, which is close to the waterfront, is a must-visit for seafood lovers. Visitors get the chance to observe the bustling market for freshly caught fish and seafood, and they may even enjoy regional specialties at neighbouring eateries.

- **Iconic Landmarks:** The Corniche and Mutrah Harbor are located close to a number of famous sites. The forts of Al Jalali and Al Mirani, built on steep cliffs and overlooking the port, add to the area's appeal by acting as silent sentinels.

- **Evening strolls:** In the evenings, when the neighbourhood comes to life with subtle lighting and a nice sea air, the Corniche and Mutrah Harbor are especially charming. A magnificent setting for a nighttime stroll is created by the illuminated buildings, busy promenade, and dynamic mood.

- Visitors may take in the traditional Omani architecture on exhibit in the buildings and structures that line the Corniche. The area's charm is enhanced by the fusion of traditional and modern elements, which also symbolises Oman's architectural history.

- **Chances for Photography:** The Corniche and Mutrah Harbor provide a wealth of chances for photographers. There are many stunning moments to be found, from catching the mesmerising sunsets over the water to capturing the brilliant colours and busy activities.

- **Relaxation & recreation:** There are many chances for outdoor activities along the Corniche, such as jogging, cycling, or just finding a place to sit and take in the tranquil atmosphere. Along the shoreline, visitors will also discover a variety of cafes and restaurants where they may enjoy Omani cuisine or a cup of authentic Omani coffee.

In addition to serving as a portal to Oman's nautical past, the Corniche and Mutrah Harbor are a bustling and welcoming destination for tourists looking for a mix of scenic beauty, cultural experiences, and leisure activities.

COASTAL DELIGHTS

Breathtaking Beaches of Oman

Oman is well known for its magnificent beaches, which have pristine coasts, clear waters, and scenic scenery. Here are a few of Oman's breathtaking beaches for you to explore:

- **Qurum Beach** is a well-liked destination for both locals and tourists alike. It is situated right in the centre of Muscat. It has a calm and welcoming ambiance thanks to its beautiful white beach, clear waters, and palm-lined promenade.

- **Al Mughsail Beach**, which is located near Salalah, is renowned for its imposing cliffs, blowholes, and immaculate sandy shoreline. This seaside treasure is enhanced by the caverns and natural rock structures.

- **Al Fazayah Beach:** With its tranquil atmosphere and breath-taking views, Al Fazayah Beach, which is close to Muscat, is a hidden gem. It is the ideal area for swimming, snorkelling, and resting due to its remote setting and clean waters.

- **Ras al-Jinz Turtle Reserve** is a must-see location for wildlife enthusiasts even though it isn't a conventional sandy beach. Visitors can experience the spellbinding sight of these magnificent creatures coming ashore to lay their eggs at this nesting location for endangered green turtles.

- **As Sawadi Beach:** To the northwest of Muscat, As Sawadi Beach is a tranquil haven. It has golden sand, quiet waves, and a peaceful ambiance, making it perfect for water sports, picnics, and sunbathing.

- **Qurum Beach's** neighbour, Shatti al-Qurum Beach, is another lovely beach with a livelier and more energetic vibe. It is a wonderful location for seaside dining and entertainment because it has a long stretch of sand bordered by opulent hotels, eateries, and cafes.

- **Bandar Jissah:** This remote beach, which is close to Muscat, is renowned for its crystal-clear seas and breathtaking natural settings. It offers a peaceful retreat from the city and provides chances for diving, snorkelling, and relaxing by the beach.

- **Marjan Beach** is well-known for its immaculate white sand, clear waves, and palm-lined coastlines. It is located in the picturesque coastal town of Salalah. It offers an opportunity to relax in the splendour of nature and a tranquil escape.

- **Tiwi Beach:** Tucked away amid soaring cliffs and crystal-clear waters in the Al Sharqiyah region, Tiwi Beach is a hidden gem. It provides a tranquil and isolated environment that is perfect for swimming, snorkelling, and sunbathing.

- **Al Waha, Al Bandar, and Al Husn** are three magnificent beaches that can be found at the Barr al Jissah beach complex, which is close to Muscat. Every beach has its own special charm, from kid-friendly activities to opulent resorts and secluded coves.

Oman's stunning beaches provide an idyllic refuge, whether you're looking for leisure, water activities, or simply the enjoyment of soaking in unspoiled natural beauty. Along Oman's breathtaking coastline, travellers can choose their ideal piece of paradise because each beach has its own distinct qualities.

Ras Al Jinz Turtle Reserve

On Oman's eastern coast, close to the town of Sur, is the exceptional conservation area known as the Ras Al Jinz Turtle Reserve. Here are some details on this unusual and fascinating location:

- **Nesting habitat for Endangered Turtles**: The endangered green turtle (Chelonia mydas) relies heavily on the Ras Al Jinz Turtle Reserve as a nesting habitat. It offers these majestic birds a haven where they can safely deposit their eggs.

- Green turtles perform their nesting procedures every night, giving visitors the amazing chance to observe them. In order to witness the turtles as they emerge from the water, make their way ashore, dig their nests, and lay their eggs, guided trips are scheduled at night. It's a beautiful and mesmerising sight to see.

- **Turtle Hatching Experience:** Depending on the season, guests may also get to see baby turtles hatch and make their way to the sea. It is an incredible experience to see these tiny animals make their way to the sea.

- **Guided Tours and Interpretive Center:** The reserve has educated guides who lead guided tours that offer insights into the biology, behaviour, and sea turtle conservation activities. Additionally offering educational exhibits and details about the turtles and their habitat is the on-site Interpretive Center.

- **Efforts in Sea Turtle Conservation and Research:** Ras Al Jinz Turtle Reserve is actively involved in sea turtle conservation and research projects. The reserve is essential to the worldwide conservation efforts for these imperilled species by monitoring and defending turtle populations.

- Ecologically sound measures are used in the reserve to lessen its negative effects on breeding turtles and their habitat. To safeguard the protection of the turtles and their nesting locations, visitors must abide by the rules.

- In addition to the turtles, the area is surrounded by breathtaking natural scenery. The Arabian Sea's turquoise waters, rugged cliffs, and immaculate beach combine to offer a beautiful scene for tourists to enjoy.

- **Cultural Connections:** Ras Al Jinz Turtle Reserve also provides information about Oman's history and regional culture. The reserve provides cultural events and activities that let guests take part in authentic Omani customs like music, dancing, and cuisine.

- **Accommodations and Facilities**: The reserve offers cosy lodging alternatives for travellers who want to spend the night and thoroughly immerse themselves in the experience of turtle conservation. A café, a gift store, and a visitor centre are additional amenities.

- **Nature and Wildlife:** The reserve is home to a variety of wildlife, including migrating birds, marine life, and rare plant species, in addition to the turtles. Visitors can learn about the reserve's many ecosystems and wildlife by exploring it.

A once-in-a-lifetime chance to see turtle nesting and hatching is provided by Ras Al Jinz Turtle Reserve. It offers a worthwhile experience that integrates education, wildlife conservation, and the opportunity to engage with Oman's natural and cultural heritage.

Wahiba Sands and Wadi Bani Khalid

Each of Oman's two compelling natural beauties, Wahiba Sands and Wadi Bani Khalid, offers a singular and unforgettable experience. What you should know about these amazing places is as follows:

Sands of Wahiba

- **Huge Desert**: Wahiba Sands, also called Sharqiya Sands, is a sizable desert that covers an area of about 12,500 square kilometres. It features impressive sand dunes that range in hue from golden to amber and form a captivating environment.

- **Dune-bashing and Desert Safaris:** Wahiba Sands is a well-liked location for dune-bashing excursions and desert safaris. Visitors get the opportunity to experience exhilarating 4x4 off-road drives under the guidance of skilled drivers who negotiate the difficult terrain and mount the magnificent sand dunes.

- The Bedouin people, who have maintained their traditional way of life, live in the desert. The chance to connect with Bedouin villages allows visitors to learn about their culture, traditions, and way of life as nomads.

- Wahiba Sands is home to a number of desert campgrounds that provide tourists an opportunity to experience the seclusion and serenity of the desert. These camps offer cosy lodging, typical cuisine, and cultural pursuits like camel rides, stargazing, and performances of regional music and dance.

- **Camel Trekking**: Camel trekking through the Wahiba Sands is a well-liked activity. Visitors can travel the undulating dunes on top of these friendly animals at a slow speed while taking in the tranquillity of the desert.

Bani Khalid Wadi

- **Oasis in the Desert:** The gorgeous oasis of Wadi Bani Khalid is located in the Eastern Hajar Mountains. With its emerald-green ponds, palm trees, and rocky cliffs, it stands out and provides a welcome contrast to the dry desert environment.

- **Natural Swimming Pools:** The wadi is home to multiple freshwater spring-fed natural swimming pools. In the midst of the spectacular grandeur of the granite canyon walls and lush vegetation, visitors can swim in the crystal-clear waters.

- **Exploration and Hiking**: Wadi Bani Khalid provides hiking options for nature lovers. The wadi is traversed by trails that reveal secluded nooks, granite formations, and breathtaking vistas. The wadi can be explored on foot for a close-up look at its natural splendours.

- **Picnic and Relaxation**: The wadi offers excellent locations for picnics and leisure activities. Visitors can have lunch while soaking in the serene atmosphere and picturesque views in the shaded areas beneath palm palms, which provide relief from the sun.

- **Activities for Adventure Seekers**: Wadi Bani Khalid offers a variety of activities. For those looking for an adrenaline rush amidst the grandeur of nature, the wadi offers opportunity for rock climbing or cliff jumping into the deep pools.

The contrasting features of Oman's natural scenery are on display in both Wahiba Sands and Wadi Bani Khalid. These locations offer remarkable experiences that highlight the nation's varied and alluring nature, from the immense desert expanse and thrilling dune bashing in Wahiba Sands to the verdant oasis and tranquil ponds of Wadi Bani Khalid.

Sur: A Coastal Gem

Sur, a coastal jewel on Oman's east coast, is a beautiful blend of the country's natural beauty, rich history, and cultural heritage. What makes Sure a fascinating place to visit is as follows:

- Sur's extensive nautical history dates back to the time when it was a thriving port for trade and shipbuilding. The city has a long history of producing ships, particularly wooden shows, which are classic sailing ships. Visitors can take in the craftsmanship and discover the complex methods utilised to build shows.

- **Sur Corniche:** Stretching down the coast, the Sur Corniche is a charming waterfront promenade that provides breathtaking views of the ocean and the city's cityscape. It's the ideal location for a stroll, offering chances for relaxing, taking in the sea wind, and taking stunning pictures.

- **Sur Nautical Museum:** The Sur Maritime Museum showcases traditional boats, instruments for navigation, and artefacts associated with Oman's nautical past. It offers insights into the city's maritime history. It's a fascinating location to discover Sur's relationship with the sea.

- **Turtle Watching in Ras Al Jinz**: Sur is the starting point for trips to the renowned Ras Al Jinz Turtle Reserve, where tourists can see how endangered green turtles lay their eggs and hatch their young. You get the chance to see these magnificent animals in their natural environment thanks to this special encounter.

- The Sur Castle and Fort, often referred to as Bilad Sur Castle, is a historic site that offers a view of the city. It is a reminder of Sur's lengthy history and dates back to the sixteenth century. Panoramas of the cityscape and the Arabian Sea may be seen from the castle.

- The Sur Old Town is a tangle of winding lanes and typical Omani architecture that offers an insight into the past of the city. Visitors can enjoy the charm of the historic homes, bustling souks, and regional craftsmanship by taking a stroll through the old neighbourhood.

- Another old fortification worth visiting is Sunaysilah Fort, which is close to Sur. This well-maintained fortress gives panoramic views of the surroundings and a look into Oman's defensive architecture.

- **Beaches in Sur**: Sur is home to lovely sandy beaches where tourists may unwind, swim, or simply enjoy the sunshine. The tranquil shoreline offers a tranquil haven and an opportunity to take in the Arabian Sea's magnificence.

- **Workshops for Dhow Construction**: Sur is known for its dhow construction business, and tourists can tour the facilities where expert craftsmen construct these traditional boats. It's a chance to see how these wooden boats, which have been important in Oman's nautical history, are made in a complex manner.

- **Traditional Omani Culture:** Sur enables guests to fully experience Omani hospitality and culture. You can sample traditional Omani food, explore neighbourhood markets, and talk to hospitable residents who are happy to share their traditions and customs.

The mix of Sur's natural beauty, historical sites, and cultural legacy make it an alluring tourist destination. Sur offers a wonderful and educational experience, whether you're interested in learning about the city's nautical past, unwinding on its immaculate beaches, or encountering the warmth of Omani culture.

Coast Road Trip: Muscat to Salalah

In Oman, setting out on a coastal road drive from Muscat to Salalah is an adventure replete with beautiful scenery, varied terrain, and intriguing sites. A proposed route for your seaside road excursion is provided below:

Muscat to Sur on Day 1

- Leave Muscat and travel toward Sur in the southeast.
- Visit the Sur Maritime Museum, take a tour of Sur's ancient town, and see how traditional shows are constructed.
- Take a stroll along the Sur Corniche and taste some local cuisine that features fresh seafood.
- Sleep there at night.

Day 2: Ras Al Jinz to Sur

- Visit the historic Sunaysilah Fort close to Sur first thing in the morning.
- As you go south down the coast, stop sometimes to take in the beautiful Arabian Sea scenery.
- Join a guided tour after arriving at Ras Al Jinz Turtle Reserve to see the green turtles nesting and hatching procedures.
- Spend the night at Ras Al Jinz or a local hotel.

Ras Al Jinz to Ras Al Hadd and Ras Al Ruwais on Day 3

- Travel south from Ras Al Jinz in the direction of the charming cities of Ras al Hadd and Ras al Ruwais.
- Visit some of the area's stunning beaches, including Al Hadd Beach and Al Mughsail Beach.

- Discover the coastal landscape's craggy cliffs, blowholes, and natural caverns.
- Ras al Hadd or Ras al Ruwais is where you spend the night.

Day 4: Salalah to Ras al Hadd

- Continue travelling south toward Salalah, the region of Dhofar's capital.
- Enjoy the beautiful trip down the coast as you travel through quaint fishing towns and coastal villages.
- Arrive at Salalah and discover the city's top attractions, such as the lively Haffa Souq, Sultan Qaboos Mosque, and Al Baleed Archaeological Park.
- Enjoy a stroll around Salalah Corniche while taking in the expansive vistas of the Arabian Sea.
- Stay the night at Salalah.

Day 5: Tour Salalah and the Area

- The Salalah region's natural attractions can be explored during the day.
- Visit the stunning Wadi Darbat, which is well-known for its verdant landscape, waterfalls, and wildlife.
- Discover the peaceful and beautiful Ayn Razat, a park in the wilderness with picnic areas and running streams.
- Explore the distinctive terrain of the renowned Qara Mountains and be in awe of the breathtaking vistas.
- Stay the night at Salalah.

Day 6: Mughsail Beach and Fazayah Beach from Salalah

- From Salalah, travel westward toward Mughsail Beach.

- Discover Mughsail Beach, which is renowned for its rocky structures and blowholes.
- Visit Fazayah Beach, a remote beach with pristine conditions renowned for its turquoise seas and sandy shoreline.
- Spend a leisurely day at the beach swimming, having a picnic, or just lazing around.
- Spend the night close to Mughsail Beach or go back to Salalah.

7th day: Departure

- Depending on when you depart, you can spend the morning lounging on one of Salalah's lovely beaches or continuing your exploration of the city.
- Leave Salalah and return to Muscat, or continue travelling and discovering more of Oman.

Please keep in mind that this schedule is only a suggestion that you might change according to your interests and free time. Before starting your coastal road trip, make sure your car is dependable, that you have adequate water and snacks for the drive, and that you have checked the weather and road conditions.

MAJESTIC MOUNTAINS

Jebel Shams: The Grand Canyon of Oman

Jebel Shams, also referred to as the "Grand Canyon of Oman," is a magnificent mountain range in Oman's Al Hajar Mountains. What makes Jebel Shams a must-see location is listed below:

- Jebel Shams offers spectacular vistas and imposing scenery reminiscent of the Grand Canyon. Spectacular Scenic Beauty. Visitors are in awe of the magnificence of nature as they take in the breathtakingly magnificent landscape created by the craggy cliffs, deep valleys, and enormous gorges.

- Jebel Shams, Oman's tallest mountain, rises impressively above sea level to a height of about 3,009 metres (9,872 feet), making it the highest peak in the country. Its imposing presence affords expansive vistas of the valleys and mountains around.

- Oman's Grand Canyon, the Wadi Ghul, is one of Jebel Shams' most recognizable features. It is also known as Oman's Grand Canyon. It offers a stunning view and an unmatched trekking experience because of its sheer cliffs that descend to a depth of about 1,000 metres (3,280 feet).

- **Trails for Hiking and Trekking:** Jebel Shams is a hiking and outdoor enthusiast's dream. The mountain range has a number of hiking and trekking trails for people of all skill levels. The most well-known is the Balcony Walk, a path that contours the canyon's rim and offers breathtaking views of the Wadi Ghul.

- Watching the sunrise or sunset from Jebel Shams is an absolutely amazing experience. You can observe the sky blazing with brilliant hues as the sun rises or sets over the huge canyon scenery thanks to the mountain peak's unhindered views.

- **Remote & Calm Ambiance:** When compared to other tourist spots in Oman, Jebel Shams is comparatively less congested. This gives the area a feeling of serenity and solitude, making it the ideal escape for people looking for a quiet, off-the-beaten-path experience.

- **Camping and stargazing:** Jebel Shams has fantastic camping areas where guests can spend the night looking up at the night sky. It's the perfect location for stargazing because of the dark, clear skies, and no light pollution, which allows you to see the Milky Way and other constellations.

- **Rock Climbing and Via Ferrata:** Jebel Shams offers rock climbing and Via Ferrata (iron route) activities for adventure seekers. Climbers get an adrenaline-pumping opportunity to test their abilities on the treacherous cliffs and difficult rock formations.

- **Cultural Encounters:** Al Hamra and Misfat Al Abriyeen, two adjacent villages, provide an insight into the traditional Omani way of life. Ancient mud-brick homes, conventional falaj irrigation systems, and the welcoming hospitality of the local residents are all open to visitors.

- **Nature and wildlife:** A wide variety of flora and fauna can be found in Jebel Shams. Watch for unusual plant types and occasional wildlife sightings, such as mountain goats and other bird species, while you explore the mountain routes.

Jebel Shams is a natural wonder that displays the captivating landscapes of Oman with its breathtaking beauty and rugged charm. Jebel Shams will forever be etched in your vacation memories, whether you're an adventurer, a nature enthusiast, or just searching for a spot to relax amidst breathtaking scenery.

Jebel Akhdar:The Green Mountain

A stunning and attractive mountain range, Jebel Akhdar, popularly known as the "Green Mountain," is situated in Oman's Al Hajar Mountains. Here are some reasons to visit Jebel Akhdar:

- The name Jebel Akhdar comes from the profusion of flora that covers its slopes. It also has terraced gardens. Numerous "aflaj," or terraced gardens, can be found across the mountain range, where local farmers grow a wide range of commodities such as pomegranates, apricots, roses, and walnuts. The vivid green landscapes provide a captivating spectacle by standing in stark contrast to the parched surroundings.

- **Pleasant Climate:** Jebel Akhdar has a colder climate than the surrounding areas because of its greater elevation.

It is the ideal hideaway during the hot summer months because of the moderate temperatures, which provide a cool retreat from the heat.

- **Saiq Plateau:** One of Jebel Akhdar's features is the Saiq Plateau. The plateau, which is located at a height of around 2,000 metres (6,500 feet), provides sweeping views of the mountains, terraced gardens, and deep valleys that surround it. Princess Diana, who visited the area, inspired the name Diana's Point, which offers a breathtaking view of the surroundings.

- **Jebel Akhdar** offers a variety of hiking and wildlife routes that let tourists get up close and personal with the mountain's stunning splendour. The trails offer an immersive experience in the hilly landscape as they lead you past terraced gardens, towns, and wadis (valleys).

- Jebel Akhdar is famed for its rose gardens, where Damask roses are raised for their fragrant petals. Rose gardens also produce rose water. The air is thick with the delicious scent of roses during the flowering season, which typically lasts from March to May. The traditional method of producing rosewater, a key component of Omani cuisine and perfumery, is open to visitors.

- Traditional Omani villages may be found all around Jebel Akhdar, providing an insight into the nation's rich cultural legacy. Discover the historic falaj irrigation systems, winding streets, and mud-brick homes. Interact with the welcoming inhabitants to learn about their customs and traditions.

- **Adventure Activities:** Jebel Akhdar offers off-road driving, mountain biking, and rock climbing for adventure seekers. The untamed mountainous environment offers exhilarating chances for outdoor excursions amidst the breathtaking scenery.

- **Wadi Bani Habib:** This gorgeous wadi (valley), which is close to Jebel Akhdar, is well-known for its terraced gardens, historic ruins, and traditional settlements. The wadi's calm atmosphere is perfect for picnics and leisurely walks.

- Another undiscovered gem is the settlement of Birkat Al-Mawz, which is close to Jebel Akhdar. It offers a real look into rural life in Omani, with its date plantations, traditional architecture, and historic ruins.

- **Stargazing**: Jebel Akhdar is a great place to go stargazing because of its secluded location and the magnificent night skies. A clear night's view of the brilliant stars above the gorgeous mountains is enchanting and unforgettably memorable.

The picturesque features of Jebel Akhdar are its traditional towns, verdant scenery, and tranquil mountain air. A trip to Jebel Akhdar guarantees a fascinating and enlightening experience, whether you're looking for natural beauty, cultural immersion, or outdoor experiences.

Al Hajar Mountain Range

A magnificent and untamed mountain range called the Al Hajar Mountain Range crosses northern Oman and the eastern United Arab Emirates. The Al Hajar Mountains' main characteristics and highlights are listed below:

- A natural marvel, the Al Hajar Mountains are made up of high cliffs, deep valleys, and towering limestone and granite summits. The range is a geological and natural history enthusiast's paradise because it is thought to have developed approximately 65 million years ago.

- The tallest mountain in the Al Hajar Mountains, Jebel Shams, is frequently referred to as the "Mountain of the Sun." It rises to a height of roughly 3,009 metres (9,872 feet), providing amazing views over the valleys and canyons in the area. The well-known

Wadi Ghul, commonly referred to as Oman's Grand Canyon, is located in Jebel Shams.

- **Jebel Akhdar:** The "Green Mountain," also known as Jebel Akhdar, is a notable feature of the Al Hajar Mountains. The region's dry landscapes arc in sharp contrast to Jebel Akhdar's terraced gardens, historic communities, and temperate climate. It is renowned for its beautiful hiking paths, fruit orchards, and rose gardens.

- **Outdoor Activities:** For adventure seekers, the Al Hajar Mountains provide a wide range of outdoor activities. There are several possibilities to explore the rough terrain and challenge yourself amidst stunning landscapes, from hiking and trekking to mountain biking and rock climbing.

- **Traditional Omani Villages**: Traditional Omani villages that offer a look into the nation's rich heritage can be found sporadically around the Al Hajar Mountains. Ancient mud-brick homes, falaj irrigation systems, and a style of life that has essentially not altered for centuries may all be found in the villages of Misfat Al Abriyeen, Al Hamra, and Wadi Bani Habib.

- **Natural Wonders**: The Al Hajar Mountains are home to a number of captivating natural wonders. The area offers a variety of picturesque landscapes to explore and enjoy, from deep wadis (valleys) like Wadi Tiwi and Wadi Shab to breathtaking rock formations like Jebel Misht and Jebel Qahwan.

- **Wildlife and Flora:** The Al Hajar Mountains' rough topography is home to a wide variety of plants and animals. Watch out for the native wild goat known as the Arabian tahr as well as various bird and reptile species. A variety of plant life, including rare and endemic species, can be found in the highlands.

- **Cultural Heritage**: Omani history and culture are closely entwined with the Al Hajar Mountains. The abundance of mediaeval forts, castles, and watchtowers in the area is a reflection of the mountains' historical importance as strategic vantage points and trading routes.

- **Stargazing**: The Al Hajar Mountains provide great stargazing opportunities due to their secluded location and low levels of light pollution. It's the perfect location for astronomy enthusiasts since on clear evenings, the dark skies reveal a captivating display of stars.

- **Scenic Drives:** The Al Hajar Mountains are a scenic drive in and of themselves. The drive is interspersed with lovely villages, scenic wadis, and breathtaking landscapes, and the hilly roads provide breathtaking views at every turn.

A magnificent natural treasure, the Al Hajar Mountain Range offers a unique blend of untamed beauty, historical significance, and outdoor adventures. A trip to the Al Hajar Mountains is certain to create a lasting impact, whether you're looking for beautiful scenery, cultural immersion, or exhilarating activities.

Nizwa: Cultural Hub of the Mountains

The historic city of Nizwa also referred to as the "Cultural Hub of the Mountains," is situated in Oman at the base of the Al Hajar Mountains. A compelling fusion of history, culture, and natural beauty can be found in Nizwa, a city renowned for its rich cultural legacy and architectural marvels. Here are some of Nizwa's highlights:

- The recognizable Nizwa Fort is a monument to the city's historical importance. One of Oman's most popular tourist destinations is this enormous fortification that was constructed in the 17th century. Discover the city's unique architecture, climb the tower for sweeping views, and discover its fascinating past.

- **Nizwa Souq:** The lively market Locals and visitors alike congregate at

Nizwa Souq to take in the lively ambiance and shop for traditional handicrafts, ceramics, silverware, spices, and other regional goods. A traditional component of Omani culture is displayed at the well-known Friday cattle market, where animal auctions are held.

- **Nizwa Grand Mosque:** Take in the spectacular grandeur of this wonderful house of worship, which showcases traditional Omani style. The elaborate sculptures, stunning dome, and serene atmosphere of this important religious landmark will awe visitors.

- **Falaj Daris:** Nizwa is renowned for its historic falaj irrigation system, which is essential for maintaining agricultural operations in the area. Investigate the Falaj Daris, a system of waterways that carries water throughout the city and the date palm groves that surround it. UNESCO has designated this system as a World Heritage Site.

- **Jebel Akhdar:** Nizwa is a point of entry to the "Green Mountain" region of Jebel Akhdar, where tourists can explore the area and see the terraced gardens, rose plantations, and traditional villages that make up the "Green Mountain." Take advantage of the colder weather, explore the area's picturesque paths, and take in the natural beauty of the surroundings.

- **Crafts:** Nizwa is renowned for its talented craftspeople who continue the traditions of ceramics, weaving, and silversmithing. Discover the city's craft studios and see for yourself the intricate processes used to make lovely handmade products.

- Nizwa holds several cultural festivals throughout the year that highlight Omani culture through music, dancing, and traditional arts. These celebrations offer a chance to become fully immersed in the community, enjoy genuine Omani cuisine, and take in traditional entertainment.

- **Jabrin Castle:** The Jabrin Castle is a stunning architectural wonder located not far from Nizwa. This well-preserved castle, which dates to the 17th century, has delicate woodwork, lovely ceiling paintings, and decorative embellishments that provide a look into the splendour of the past.

- **Al Hoota Cave:** Visit the captivating underground environment of this cave close to Nizwa. Stunning stalactites, stalagmites, and underground lakes can be seen during a guided tour of the caves, which are a spellbinding natural wonder.

- **Excursions to Jebel Shams:** From Nizwa, you can travel to Jebel Shams, also referred to as the "Mountain of the Sun." Experience the Grand Canyon of Oman's spectacular views, stroll along picturesque pathways, and engage in outdoor activities in this magnificent mountainous location.

Travellers looking for an authentic Omani experience will find Nizwa to be a captivating destination thanks to its rich cultural heritage, stunning architecture, and proximity to natural wonders. Discover its ancient landmarks, spend time in its authentic markets, and take in the lively ambiance of this cultural centre in the Alps.

Jebel Al Misht: A Trekker Paradise

In Oman's Al Hajar Mountain Range, Jebel Al Misht is a trekker's paradise that offers exhilarating thrills and breathtakingly beautiful scenery. For those who enjoy trekking, Jebel Al Misht is a must-visit location:

- Jebel Al Misht, popularly referred to as "The Comb," is one of the majestic peaks in the Al Hajar Mountains. It rises to a height of roughly 1,829 metres (6,001 feet), providing stunning panoramas of the surrounding scenery, including the deep valleys and rocky mountain ranges.

- Jebel Al Misht is renowned for its difficult hiking routes, which draw seasoned hikers looking for an exhilarating outdoor adventure. There is a sense of success and an adrenaline rush to be had from the trip to the summit, which encompasses steep hills, rocky terrain, and winding pathways.

- Beautiful scenery can be seen as you climb Jebel Al Misht, which is surrounded by craggy cliffs, narrow gorges, and unusual rock formations. Along the trip, you'll come across vibrant plants, such as wildflowers and bushes, which bring some beauty to the arid environment.

- **Geological Wonders:** The Jebel Al Misht mountain range, which is part of the Al Hajar Mountains, is a geological wonder that displays millions of years of geological activity. You can see intriguing rock formations, such as limestone and granite formations, as you hike through the mountain. These forms were created throughout time by natural processes.

- **Wildlife Encounters:** The rough mountain environment of Jebel Al Misht is home to a variety of wildlife species that flourish there. Watch out for the wild goat-like Arabian tahr, as well as other bird, reptile, and bug species that call the area home.

- **Remote & Untouched Nature:** Jebel Al Misht offers a sense of seclusion and calmness that makes it possible to commune with nature in its most unadulterated state. You can immerse yourself in the tranquil surroundings, breathe in the pure mountain air, and enjoy the serenity of the woods away from the activity and noise of the city.

- Excellent camping opportunities can be found in Jebel Al Misht for hikers.

Set up camp in a beautiful area, take in the starry night sky, and awaken to the tranquil sounds of nature. For outdoor enthusiasts, camping amidst Jebel Al Misht's untamed beauty is a wonderful experience.

- **Adventure Photography:** Jebel Al Misht provides many options for adventure photography with its breathtaking scenery and dramatic panoramas. Take pictures of the untamed beauty, unusual rock formations, and expansive views as you travel through them.

- **Exploration of Culture:** The Omani culture and legacy are strongly present in the area surrounding Jebel Al Misht. Visit some of the adjacent traditional villages and talk to the residents there to learn about their culture, traditions, and customs.

- **Sense of Achievement**: Climbing Jebel Al Mishti's difficult routes and reaching the peak gives one a tremendous sense of achievement. Your efforts are rewarded by the stunning views at the summit, which leave you with enduring memories of an incredible trekking adventure.

Trekkers can go on a thrilling and difficult expedition on Jebel Al Misht while taking in the Al Hajar Mountains' untamed splendour. As you explore this trekker's paradise, immerse yourself in the natural wilderness, take in breathtaking views, and embrace the spirit of adventure.

DESERT ADVENTURES

Wahiba Sands: A Desert Expedition

A mesmerising desert location in Oman known as Wahiba Sands, Sharqiyah Sands, or Wahiba Desert entices travellers to go out on exhilarating desert expeditions. Here are some reasons to visit Wahiba Sands if you want to have a distinctive desert experience:

- Huge, untouched areas of sand dunes can be seen in Wahiba Sands, stretching as far as the eye can reach. A captivating environment that is both awe-inspiring and strange is made up of the golden-hued dunes that vary in size and shape.

- **Desert camping**: One of the highlights of any trip to Wahiba Sands is a night spent beneath the starry desert sky. Camp in authentic Bedouin tents, take advantage of the warm hospitality of the locals, and spend a peaceful evening amidst the calm desert atmosphere.

- Wahiba Sands is an off-road enthusiast's delight, offering dune stomping and desert drives. Join a spectacular dune bashing trip where expert drivers in 4x4 vehicles provide an exhilarating and thrilling journey through the steep dunes.

- **Camel Trekking:** Take a classic camel trip to savour the grandeur of the desert. Take a ride over the undulating dunes, take in the tranquillity of the desert, and get to know the Bedouin people, who have survived in this hostile environment for thousands of years.

- Experience the rush of sliding down the sand-covered hills on a sandboard or a pair of sand skis. The dunes at Wahiba Sands make the ideal setting for these thrilling sports, letting you slide down the slopes and experience an adrenaline rush.

- Wahiba Sands is the home of the Bedouin people, who have adapted to the desert climate and maintained their ancient way of life. Bedouin culture and hospitality. Participate in local Bedouin communities, discover their culture, traditions, and tales, and enjoy typical Omani cuisine.

- **Desert wildlife:** Despite the desert's apparent lack of life, Wahiba Sands is home to a remarkable variety of plants and fauna that have adapted to the desert environment. Be on the lookout for animals that have adapted to survive in this harsh environment, such as Arabian oryx, sand gazelles, desert foxes, and many bird species.

- **Sunrises and Sunsets:** It is a magnificent experience to watch the desert change as the sun rises or sets in a golden tint. The sand's colours shift as the sun descends into the horizon or rises over the dunes, producing an astounding display of the beauty of nature.

- **Starry Nights:** Wahiba Sands' secluded position and low levels of light pollution provide ideal observing conditions. The desert sky transforms into a celestial show on clear nights, with innumerable stars lining the night sky and constellations flashing brightly above.

- **Desert quiet and Serenity**: Wahiba Sands is a singular chance to escape the contemporary world and immerse oneself in the quiet and serenity of the desert. You can refresh your thoughts, get lost in the simplicity of desert life, and take in the splendour of nature thanks to the landscape's vastness and seclusion.

Adventurers are invited to explore the fascinating world of the sand dunes, take part in exhilarating desert activities, and become immersed in the rich culture and peacefulness of the desert at Wahiba Sands. The Wahiba Sands offer the chance to embark on an extraordinary journey into the heart of Oman's desert wilderness.

Bedouin Culture and Hospitality

The hospitality and culture of the Bedouin are fundamental to the history and way of life of the Arabs, including in Oman. The Bedouins are a nomadic Arab clan that has historically lived in Oman's Wahiba Sands and other desert areas. Here's a look at Bedouin culture and the welcoming welcome they give guests:

- Bedouins lead a nomadic lifestyle, travelling in search of water and grazing areas with their herds of camels, goats, and sheep. They have a strong bond with the desert and rely on their understanding of it to survive in the hostile environment.

- **Traditions around hospitality:** Bedouin hospitality is renowned. In Bedouin villages, guests are treated kindly, with respect, and with charity. Bedouin hospitality includes sharing meals, conversing with guests, and sipping tea or Arabic coffee.

- **Majlis**: Referring to "a place of sitting," the Majlis is a crucial part of Bedouin culture. It describes a place where people congregate to socialise, tell stories, talk about pressing issues, and show hospitality to visitors. It stands for community and harmony.

- **Traditional Food and Drink:** The austerity of Bedouin nomadic existence is often reflected in their cuisine. Mandi (slow-cooked pork and rice), shuwa (marinated and roasted lamb), and various flatbreads are examples of traditional fare. A look into the Bedouins' culinary customs can be obtained by dining with them.

- **Bedouin Crafts and abilities:** Over the course of many generations, Bedouins have developed a variety of crafts and abilities. These include metalwork, weaving, embroidery, rug-making, and pottery. The exquisite motifs on bedouin items showcase their culture's artistic traditions.

- Bedouin men typically dress in a long, loose-fitting robe called a thobe or dishdasha, while women typically don a black abaya and a facial veil known as a niqab. Bedouin clothing shields wearers from the elements and expresses the community's culture.

- Bedouin dancing and music are lively representations of their culture. Traditional music and dances are accompanied by rhythmic tunes played on instruments including the oud (a stringed instrument), rebaba (a spike violin), and tabla (a drum).

- **Stories & Oral Traditions:** The Bedouin people have a long legacy of oral history and storytelling. They transmit their culture through stories, folklore, and poems, maintaining their history, cultural traditions, and understanding of the desert environment.

- Camels are prized in Bedouin culture because they are necessary companions and modes of transportation in the desert. The importance of camels in supporting the Bedouin way of life and their intimate awareness of their care is evident.

- **Cultural encounters:** Interacting with Bedouin culture offers tourists a singular and genuine experience. A deeper understanding of the Bedouin way of life and a greater appreciation for culture can be gained by participating in traditional camel treks, staying in a Bedouin camp, or taking part in cultural exchange programs.

The hospitality and culture of the Bedouins provide a window into a long-standing way of life that has been moulded by the desert environment. Visitors that interact with Bedouins might witness their friendliness, generosity, and deeply ingrained customs, resulting in lifelong memories of cultural interchange and understanding.

Camel trekking and Dune-bashing

Two thrilling activities that let visitors experience the distinctive sceneries and adrenaline of the desert are camel trekking and dune bashing. What you should know about camel riding and sand boarding in Oman is as follows:

Trekking with camels

- Camel trekking is a long-standing cultural tradition in the Arabian Peninsula. It provides a look at the nomadic way of life and the traditional means of getting around in the desert.

- Camel excursions provide visitors the chance to take their time and slowly explore the expanse of the desert. You may enjoy the calm atmosphere, study the desert flora and animals, and take in the natural beauty of the surroundings by riding a camel through the sand dunes.

- **Connection to the Bedouin:** Many camel treks in Oman are accompanied by knowledgeable Bedouin leaders who impart their understanding of the desert's mysteries and cultural customs. Interacting with the Bedouins gives the encounter a richer cultural component.

- **Treks at Sunset and Sunrise:** Choosing a sunset or sunrise camel excursion will enhance the desert's visual splendour. It is a truly magnificent and unforgettable experience to watch the sunrise over the horizon or shed vivid hues over the sand dunes.

- **Camping Under the Stars**: You may truly immerse yourself in the desert experience by combining camel riding with an overnight camping trip. Enjoy a great lunch by the campfire, set up camp in a classic Bedouin-style tent, and go to sleep beneath the starry desert sky.

"Dune bashing"

- Dune bashing is an exhilarating off-road adventure that involves driving 4x4 cars across the sandy landscape of the desert, scaling steep dunes, and engaging in exhilarating manoeuvres. Professional drivers manoeuvre the difficult terrain, offering a thrilling and adrenaline-pumping trip.

- Dune bashing demands unique driving methods to overcome the soft sand and steep slopes of the desert. To provide a comfortable and secure ride, drivers use techniques include releasing tire pressure, maintaining momentum, and moving the vehicle.

- Dune bashing gives you the chance to experience breath-taking panoramic vistas of the desert. You'll get breathtaking views of the sweeping sands stretching into the distance as you climb the dunes, inspiring awe and a deeper understanding of the enormity of the desert.

- **Opportunities for Photography**: Dune bashing offers fantastic chances to take beautiful pictures. Images that are spectacular and memorable are created by the interaction of light and shadow on the dunes, the contours and textures of the sand, and the dynamic movement of the cars.

- Dune bashing is a fun and social activity because it is frequently done in groups. It enhances the overall experience to share the joy and fun with other adventurers, forging bonds of friendship and lasting memories.

- **Important Reminder**: Although camel trekking and dune-bashing are exciting activities, it's crucial to select tour companies or guides with a reputation for putting safety and environmental sustainability first. They will make sure the animals are taken care of and follow ethical standards to have the least possible negative effects on the delicate environment of the desert.

You may connect with the desert environment and make priceless memories of your time in Oman's wide and alluring landscapes by participating in either dune bashing for an adrenaline-fueled adventure or camel trekking for a more tranquil and cultural experience.

Camping in the Desert

You may connect with nature, enjoy the quiet, and take in the splendour of the desert night sky by camping in the desert, which is a fascinating and immersive experience. When organising a camping trip in Oman's desert, keep the following factors in mind:

- **Pick the Right Place:** Oman has a number of desert camping areas, including Wahiba Sands, Rub' al Khali (Empty Quarter), and Sharqiyah Sands. Considering accessibility, amenities, and the kind of desert landscape you want to enjoy, do your research and choose a place that meets your tastes.

- **Camps in the Bedouin style:** If you want a more genuine experience, think about staying in a camp in the Bedouin style. These campgrounds frequently include traditional-style tents or huts, cosy bedding, and social areas where visitors may unwind and mingle. In addition to providing cultural activities like traditional music and dance performances, bedouin camps also serve local cuisine.

- Make sure you have all the tools and materials you'll need for camping, including tents, sleeping bags, a camp stove, cooking utensils, and enough water. Camping in the desert involves careful planning and preparation because there might not be shops or facilities nearby in distant locations.

- **Weather considerations:** The desert can suffer extremely high daytime temperatures and low temperatures at night. Pack appropriate attire, such as breathable, light-weight clothing for the daytime and warm layers for the evenings when it gets cooler. Don't forget to protect yourself from the harsh desert sun by packing basics like sunscreen, hats, and sunglasses.

- **Safety Measures:** There are a few safety measures to take when camping in the desert. It's a good idea to let someone know that you're going camping, especially if you're going somewhere distant. Bring a first aid kit, a cell phone that is fully charged, and a map or GPS gadget for navigation. Learn Oman's emergency phone numbers, and heed any instructions or cautions issued by local authorities.

- Respect the fragile desert ecosystem by leaving no trace by camping safely. By correctly disposing of waste and minimising environmental harm, you can leave no trace behind. Respect wildlife and don't bother or feed any animals you come across.

- **Stargazing:** The chance to view the night sky when camping in the desert is one of its attractions. The desert sky transforms into a painting of glittering stars and constellations when there is little light pollution. Consider carrying a star map or astronomy guide to enhance your time spent awestruck by the celestial splendour.

- **Desert Activities:** In addition to taking in the peace and beauty of the desert, you might want to try camel trekking, dune-bashing, sandboarding, or just taking a leisurely stroll to get a feel for the area. Through these activities, you can develop a stronger bond with the desert ecosystem and get in touch with its spirit of exploration.

- Gather around a campfire to swap tales, have a mouthwatering BBQ, and take in the warmth of the fire. Check your area's laws regulating campfires and abide by any restrictions to avoid wildfires.

- **Accept the Experience:** Desert camping offers a chance to unplug from the daily grind and appreciate the simplicity and tranquillity of the desert. Allow the desert to reawaken your senses and renew your spirit as you immerse yourself in the silence, take in the immensity of the surroundings, and enjoy the tranquillity.

A one-of-a-kind and amazing experience, camping in the desert helps you to develop a strong bond with the natural world and the elements. Your camping trip in Oman will be an amazing and treasured memory if you come prepared, respect the environment, and appreciate the desert's natural beauty.

Al Rustaq:Hot Springs and Forts

Oman's Al Rustaq is a mediaeval town renowned for its majestic forts and hot springs. What you should know about the forts and hot springs in Al Rustaq is as follows:

Al Rustaq's thermal springs:

- Ain Al Kasfa is a well-known hot spring known for its healing effects, and it is close to the town of Al Rustaq. It is thought that the mineral-rich water in Ain Al Kasfa can treat a number of diseases. Visitors can unwind and rejuvenate while taking a swim in the warm waters.

- Al Thowarah Hot Springs: Al Thowarah, often referred to as Al Khoudh, is another noteworthy hot spring in Al Rustaq. It is a naturally hot spring surrounded by palm trees, which makes for a lovely scene. The water can be as hot as 45 degrees Celsius (113 degrees Fahrenheit), which makes for a relaxing and energising experience.

Al Rustaq forts:

- One of Oman's most impressive forts is Al Rustaq Fort, often referred to as Al Hazm Fort. This architectural wonder, which dates back to the 13th century, was home to the powerful Al Yarubi dynasty. The fort has tall towers, thick walls, and elaborate architectural features. Visit the fort's museum, explore the interior courtyards, and take in the expansive views from the elevated viewing points.

- Al Rustaq is not exactly adjacent to Nakhal Fort, but it is close enough and is worth a visit. This well-preserved fort, which is located in the adjacent village of Nakhal, was built before the advent of Islam. In addition to providing spectacular views of the nearby mountains and oasis, it provides an insight into Oman's rich history.

- Al Hazm Castle is a beautiful piece of architecture even if it is not a fort. This castle, which is close to Al Rustaq, was built in the 18th century and has elaborate stucco work and elegant timber ceilings. Discover all of its spaces, including the lobby, prayer room, and watchtowers.

Additional Attractions in Al-Rustaq

- Visit the historic souq (market) in Al Rustaq to fully experience the vivacious local culture. Spices, clothing, handmade crafts, and fresh food are just a few of the items you can browse through here. Interact with local sellers while taking in the colourful atmosphere.

- **Date Plantations in Al Rustaq**: Al Rustaq is renowned for its date palm orchards, where you can see this significant crop being grown. Explore the date plantations, discover date farming, and even try some fresh dates.

- **Al Rustaq Fort Park:** Located next to Al Rustaq Fort, the fort park offers a relaxing area for recreation. Take a stroll, have a picnic in the shade, or just relax in the peaceful setting.

The hot springs and forts of Al Rustaq offer a rare fusion of natural wonders and historic sites. This lovely town in Oman encourages you to immerse yourself in its rich cultural legacy and natural beauty, from calming hot springs to majestic fortifications.

CULTURAL HERITAGE

Bahla: UNESCO World Heritage Site

Oman's captivating town of Bahla is recognized as a UNESCO World Heritage Site, which is an honour. What you should know about Bahla and its significance is as follows:

- Bahla is renowned for having a long history, with settlements existing as early as the Bronze Age. During the Middle Ages, the town prospered as a centre for Islamic learning and pottery.

- The magnificent fort known as Bahla Fort or Hisn Tamah is the focal point of Bahla. This impressive fort made of mud bricks is one of Oman's biggest and oldest. It was built in the thirteenth century and exhibits conventional Omani design. The fort is distinguished by its high walls, protective towers, and elaborate patterns. Visitors can wander through its maze-like corridors, ascend to the top for sweeping vistas, and take in the historical artefacts on display.

- **UNESCO World Heritage Site:** In 1987, the Bahla Fort and its surrounding oasis received a joint UNESCO World Heritage Site designation. The town's exceptional universal value and cultural significance are acknowledged by this designation. The fort is a symbol of the region's architectural history and the skill of Omani artisans.

- **Pottery and craftsmanship:** Bahla is well known for its traditional craftsmanship, especially in pottery. Bahla pottery, which has a long history in the town, is known for its exquisite craftsmanship. Visitors can watch expert craftspeople mould clay and create intricate designs. The pottery is distinguished by its traditional motifs, geometric patterns, and earthy tones.

- **Bahla Souq:** Take a stroll through the crowded Bahla Souq to experience the energetic local atmosphere. The souq sells a variety of products, including traditional crafts, pottery, textiles, spices, and frankincense from the Sultanate of Oman. It's a great place to meet locals, get a taste of Omani culture, and buy unusual trinkets.

- **Bahla Oasis:** A lush oasis surrounds the town of Bahla, adding to its allure. Take a stroll through the palm groves to take in the lush surroundings and the traditional aflaj irrigation systems. The oasis serves as a reminder of the significance of water in maintaining life in the area and offers a refreshing contrast to the dry desert landscapes.

- **Cultural Festivals:** Throughout the year, Bahla hosts a number of festivals that allow tourists to take in local music, dance, and holiday performances. The Bahla Fort Festival, which brings the fort to life with cultural events and celebrates the town's history, is one noteworthy festival.

By going to Bahla, you can travel back in time and take in the allure of a historic, old town. Bahla offers a glimpse into Oman's rich cultural heritage and architectural prowess with its imposing fort, vibrant souq, and surrounding oasis.

Al Hamra:Traditional Omani village

In the middle of Oman's Al Hajar Mountain Range is the picturesque traditional Omani village of Al Hamra. What you should know about Al Hamra and its cultural significance are the following:

- Al Hamra is well known for its preserved traditional mud-brick homes, which exhibit the traditional Omani architectural style. These houses, known as "bayt al qufl," are characterised by their tall walls, narrow windows, and intricately carved wooden doors.

  Walking through the village, you'll be transported back in time as you admire the timeless beauty of the buildings and the craftsmanship that went into their construction.

- **Al-Hamra Heritage Village:** The Al-Hamra Heritage Village is a living museum that offers visitors a glimpse into the traditional Omani way of life.

  The village is a showcase of Omani heritage, with displays of traditional artefacts, tools, and household items. Visitors can explore the village, interact with locals, and learn about the customs, traditions, and history of the region.

- **Bait Al Safah Museum:** The Bait Al Safah Museum is located in the Al-Hamra Heritage Village. With the help of this museum's immersive experience, you can discover more about the Omani people's culture, traditions, and way of life. Traditional attire, jewellery, household items, and displays showcasing traditional crafts and abilities are all included in the exhibits.

- **Falaj System:** The village of Al Hamra is renowned for its sophisticated irrigation system, the falaj system, which was used to direct water from underground sources to the village's farms and orchards. This area's lush vegetation is maintained by a traditional water management system that is an essential component of Oman's agricultural heritage.

- Al Hamra serves as the entrance to Jebel Shams, Oman's tallest mountain. Visitors can enjoy panoramic views of the surrounding valleys and deep canyons while taking a scenic drive through the breath-taking mountain roads. Popular locations for outdoor pursuits like hiking, camping, and rock climbing include Jebel Shams.

- **Date Plantations in Al Hamra**: Al Hamra is renowned for its date palm groves, where tourists can see how dates are traditionally grown. The date plantations provide a tranquil setting for a leisurely stroll as well as the opportunity to sample fresh dates or buy some to take home as mementos.

- **Traditional Crafts**: The skilled artisans who practise traditional crafts like basketry, weaving, and pottery can be found in Al Hamra. Visitors are welcome to watch these artisans at work and even practise these traditional arts with their guidance.

- **Local cuisine:** In Al Hamra, you can sample genuine Omani cuisine at neighbourhood eateries. Enjoy traditional fare like shuwa (slow-cooked lamb), harees (savoury porridge), and various rice dishes with delicious flavours. Don't pass up the chance to experience the renowned Omani hospitality while sipping a cup of coffee and dates.

The opportunity to experience Oman's rich cultural heritage is exceptional when visiting Al Hamra. Al Hamra offers a memorable and immersive cultural experience and offers an authentic glimpse into the traditional Omani way of life through its traditional architecture, historical museum, and natural surroundings.

Sohar:Birthplace of Sinbad the Sailor

The legendary seafaring figure from Arabian folklore, Sinbad the Sailor, was born in Sohar, a historic city in the Sultanate of Oman. What you should know about Sohar and its connection to Sinbad is as follows:

- **Historical Importance**: Sohar has a lengthy and illustrious past that goes back to antiquity. The city served as a key trading centre for the area and was crucial to the maritime trade routes connecting the Arabian Peninsula, India, and East Africa.

- A fictional character from the "One Thousand and One Nights" (Arabian Nights) collection of tales, Sinbad the Sailor, is thought to have come from Sohar. Readers are captivated by Sinbad's tales of exploration and adventure because of his encounters with fantastical creatures, enchanted places, and dangerous sea voyages.

- Visit the purported tomb of Sinbad the Sailor in Sohar, which is known as Sinbad's Tomb. The grave is in a tiny cemetery close to the city's harbour. Even though the tomb's veracity is disputed, it is still a well-liked tourist destination and a memorial to the legendary figure.

- The Sohar Fort, also known as the Al Hazm Fort, is one of the city's most recognizable landmarks. The fort, which was constructed in the 13th century, housed the local kings and was essential in the city's defence. Today, tourists can explore the fort's impressive walls, towers, and courtyards to learn more about the historical significance of the area.

- Visit the Sohar Souq to fully experience the vivacious local culture. You can take in the bustling atmosphere here and shop for a wide range of products, including fresh produce, textiles, spices, and traditional Omani handicrafts. It's a great place to meet the locals, try the food, and see how they live traditionally.

- **Sohar Port:** One of Oman's principal ports, the Sohar Port, is located in Sohar. The port is important to Oman's economy because it promotes trade and acts as a hub for imports and exports.

- **Sohar's Coastal Appeal:** Sohar is fortunate to have a stunning coastline and immaculate beaches. Visitors can unwind on the sandy beaches, enjoy the picturesque Arabian Sea views, and engage in water sports like swimming, snorkelling, and fishing.

- **Sohar Gardens:** This city is well-known for its verdant gardens, which provide a welcome oasis in the arid terrain of Oman. Enjoy the fragrant flowers while taking a stroll through the gardens and unwinding in the shaded areas.

Exploring a city rich in history and maritime heritage while in Sohar gives you the chance to learn more about the stories surrounding Sinbad the Sailor. Sohar offers a fascinating fusion of cultural attractions and natural landscapes that will capture the imagination of any traveller, from its forts and souqs to its coastal beauty.

Omani Cuisine and Traditional Delicacies

The history, geography, and cultural diversity of Oman have all had an impact on the delicious flavour combination that is Omani cuisine. You should try the following traditional Omani foods and treats:

- **Shuwa:** Often referred to as Oman's national dish, shuwa consists of slow-cooked lamb or goat that has been marinated in a blend of spices like turmeric, coriander, and cinnamon.

  The meat is cooked in an underground sand oven for several hours while being wrapped in banana leaves to make it tender and succulent. Shuwa is a must-try dish that is typically prepared for special occasions and festivals due to its aromatic flavours.

- **Majboos/Makbous**: A flavorful rice dish made with meat (typically chicken or beef), vegetables, and a variety of spices, is known as majboos. Saffron, cardamom, and dried limes are frequently used to season rice, giving it a unique flavour and aroma. This filling and hearty dish is a favourite for celebrations and family get-togethers.

- **Harees** is a traditional Omani dish made from ground wheat and meat (usually lamb or chicken), which is cooked together until it resembles thick porridge. It is spiced, and ghee (clarified butter) and cinnamon are frequently used as garnishes. Harees is a popular dish during the holy month of Ramadan and is regarded as a filling and cosy meal.

- **Mashuai**: Mashuai is a well-known Omani dish made of whole, spiced lamb that is roasted on a spit or baked in the oven and typically served over fragrant saffron rice. The meat is given a unique flavour by being marinated in a mixture of spices that includes cumin, turmeric, and black lime. The flavorful rice and tender meat make mashuai a preferred dish for festive occasions.

- **Omani Shrimp Rice**: This dish combines tender shrimp with flavorful basmati rice, herbs, and spices, as well as saffron. The rice is cooked in the shrimp broth after being seasoned with the flavorful shrimp, which is typically seasoned with turmeric, red chilli, and garlic.

- The traditional Omani dessert known as hareesah is made with ground wheat, sugar, ghee, and flavorful spices like cardamom and rosewater. The mixture of ingredients is slowly cooked until it resembles pudding and is smooth and creamy. When there is a celebration or a special occasion, hareesa is frequently served.

- **Omani Halwa:** Popular in Omani cuisine, omani halwa is a sweet confection made with rosewater, saffron, sugar, ghee, and a variety of nuts, including almonds and cashews. Its texture is gooey and jelly-like, and it's frequently flavoured with things like rosewater, saffron, or dates. The popular dessert omani halwa is frequently provided as a sign of hospitality.

- **Dates**: In Omani cuisine, dates have a special place and are revered as a sign of hospitality. The popular khlas and medjool dates are just two of the high-quality dates that Oman is renowned for. Dates are eaten as a sweet snack on their own, with Omani coffee, or in a variety of desserts and dishes.

To fully experience Oman's rich culinary heritage, be sure to try these traditional Omani dishes and treats while you're there. Omani cuisine offers a variety of flavours that will please your palate, from hearty rice dishes to decadent desserts.

Traditional Arts and Crafts

Oman's rich cultural diversity and historical importance are reflected in the country's rich heritage of traditional arts and crafts. You can find the following traditional arts and crafts in Oman:

- **Pottery**: Oman has a long history of pottery production dating back many centuries. Beautiful clay vessels and decorative items are made by skilled artisans using age-old methods. Intricate patterns, geometric shapes, and traditional Omani motifs are frequently seen on the pottery. Pottery from Bahla and Salalah is particularly well-known.

- Another traditional craft in Oman is weaving, which is primarily used to make textiles and carpets. Handwoven textiles frequently feature complex patterns and vivid colours. Traditional Omani carpets, known as "sad," are woven vertically and feature geometric patterns influenced by local culture and the natural world.

- **Silver jewellery:** Omani silver jewellery is renowned for its dexterous craftsmanship and intricate designs. Beautiful objects, such as necklaces, bracelets, earrings, and traditional Omani Khanjars (curved daggers), are made by silversmiths. Filigree work, intricate patterns, and semi-precious stones are frequently used in jewellery.

- **Omani Khanjars:** The traditional Omani dagger, or khanjar, is a representation of the nation's culture. Khanjars have beautifully detailed handles, curved blades, and intricate finishing. Khanjars are made by skilled craftspeople with expertise in metalwork, woodworking, and engraving.

- **Palm Leaf Weaving**: The art of palm leaf weaving, also referred to as "Sadu Al Shana," uses dried palm fronds to make a variety of objects. Intricate patterns and designs are woven into mats, baskets, hats, and decorative items by skilled artisans. Thc craft of palm leaf weaving demonstrates the ingenuity and imagination of Omani artisans.

- **Metalwork and silverware**: Omani artisans are skilled at producing beautiful metalwork and silverware. Coffee pots, incense burners, trays, and decorative items are examples of traditional silverware. Traditional coffee pots and decorative plates are among the items made with copper and brass.

- **Production of Frankincense:** Oman is renowned for producing frankincense, a fragrant resin with important cultural and historical associations. Local craftspeople carry out the age-old tasks of collecting, drying, and sorting frankincense. Incense sticks, essential oils, and fragrances are just a few examples of the many uses for the resin.

- **Dhow Construction:** Dhows are conventional wooden sailing ships that have been utilised for centuries in maritime trade between Arabia and Oman. Oman still employs the craft of dhow construction, especially along the coast. These lovely wooden boats are built by skilled craftsmen using age-old methods, preserving the nation's maritime heritage.

Investigating these traditional arts and crafts in Oman offers a window into the craftsmanship and cultural heritage of the nation. Each craft exemplifies the rich artistic traditions of Oman, whether it be the intricate designs used in pottery, the weaving methods used in textiles, or the elaborate silver jewellery. It's a great idea to support and appreciate these traditional arts and crafts by going to local markets, museums, and craft galleries.

NATURAL WONDERS

Wadi Shab: The Jewel of Oman

The breathtaking natural attraction Wadi Shab, also known as the "Jewel of Oman," is situated in the country's Al Sharqiyah region. What makes Wadi Shab a must-see location is listed below:

- **Stunning Scenery:** Wadi Shab is well known for its breathtaking natural beauty. Towering cliffs, dense palm groves, and turquoise pools of crystal-clear water will greet you as you enter the wadi. A captivating scene is produced by the stark topography and the lush vegetation.

- **Swimming and Hiking:** Wadi Shab provides a special mix of swimming and hiking opportunities. Pools of emerald water can be found as you hike along the wadi's rocky trails. The hike's high point is arriving at the main pool, where you can cool off in the turquoise water. Swimming through the constrained canyon while being surrounded by cliffs is an unforgettable experience.

- **Cave exploration:** The "Majlis al Jinn" cave is one of Wadi Shab's undiscovered treasures. One of the biggest limestone caverns in the world, it can only be reached by a strenuous hike and swim. Exploring the cave offers a unique perspective on Oman's geological wonders and is an adventure all on its own.

- **Natural Rock Formations:** Throughout Wadi Shab, you'll find amazing rock formations that have been eroded by water over many years. The wadi's smooth contours, organic arches, and intricate designs carved into the rock walls add to its allure and provide fantastic photo opportunities.

- **Flora and Fauna:** A variety of plant and animal species can be found in Wadi Shab, giving nature lovers the chance to study the area's ecosystem. While exploring the wadi's trails, keep an eye out for colourful birds, dragonflies, butterflies, and the sporadic sighting of small mammals or reptiles.

- **Picnic Areas and Relaxation Areas:** Wadi Shab offers a number of picturesque areas along its banks where you can stop, have a picnic, or just unwind amidst the peace of nature. Find a spot in the shade under a palm tree, take in the calm atmosphere, and take in the tranquillity of the surroundings.

- **Opportunities for photography:** Whether you're a beginner or a seasoned photographer, Wadi Shab provides countless chances to take breathtaking pictures. Every nook of the wadi offers a picturesque scene just waiting to be captured, from the rough cliffs and cascading waterfalls to the vibrant hues of the pools and lush vegetation.

It's crucial to respect the environment when visiting Wadi Shab and to adhere to any rules or restrictions put in place to protect the area's beauty. Whether you're looking for adventure, are a fan of nature, or are just looking to relax in a breathtaking environment, Wadi Shab will leave you in awe of Oman's natural splendours.

Bimmah Sinkhole:A Geological Wonder

In Oman, close to the coastal town of Bimmah, is the remarkable geological wonder known as the Bimmah Sinkhole, also referred to as Hawiyat Najm Park. What makes the Bimmah Sinkhole such a unique place is as follows:

- **Unusual Formation:** The sinkhole was naturally created when an underground limestone cavern collapsed, leaving behind a sizable circular depression and eye-catching turquoise water. The symmetrical shape of the sinkhole and the vivid contrast between the pool and the surrounding cliffs make for an arresting sight.

- **Water That Is Crystal Clear**: The Bimmah Sinkhole is renowned for its stunningly inviting water. Freshwater from underground springs and saltwater from the nearby Gulf of Oman are combined to fill the pool. Swimmable and refreshing waters are available for visitors to enjoy, making it a memorable and rejuvenating experience.

- **Natural Setting:** The sinkhole is surrounded by craggy limestone cliffs, which give the area a remote and picturesque feel. Beautiful rock formations, lush vegetation, and small cascading waterfalls can be found in the surrounding landscape, which enhances the area's natural beauty.

- Snorkelling and diving enthusiasts will find the Bimmah Sinkhole to be the perfect location due to the crystal-clear water and excellent visibility. A vibrant marine ecosystem with colourful fish and other fascinating marine life is revealed by underwater exploration.

- The Bimmah Sinkhole has been transformed into a visitor-friendly park with amenities like covered picnic areas, seating areas, and restrooms. It provides a tranquil setting where guests can unwind, enjoy a picnic, or just take in the beauty of the surroundings.

- **Geological Significance:** The sinkhole provides a rare opportunity to observe the processes that shape the Earth's surface geologically. It sheds light on how limestone landscapes are created and eroded, demonstrating how dynamic our planet is.

- The Bimmah Sinkhole is significant from a cultural perspective for the neighbourhood. The sinkhole is known by the Arabic name Hawiyat Najm, which translates to "The Falling

Star" as local folklore holds that a falling star caused it to form. The geological marvel gains a little more mystery and intrigue as a result.

It is possible to appreciate the wonder and beauty of nature's creations by going to the Bimmah Sinkhole. The Bimmah Sinkhole offers a singular experience that highlights the geological wonders of Oman, whether you're a nature enthusiast, an adventure seeker, or just looking for a quiet place to relax.

Jebel Samhan Nature Reserve

In the southern Oman region of Dhofar, there is a breathtaking protected area called Jebel Samhan Nature Reserve. What makes Jebel Samhan Nature Reserve such a special place for nature lovers is as follows:

- **Awe-inspiring Terrain:** The nature reserve is known for its breathtaking terrain, which features towering mountains, deep canyons, and steep cliffs. The area's highest peak, Jebel Samhan, provides breathtaking panoramas of the valleys and coastline below.

- **Rich Biodiversity:** The reserve is a haven for wildlife enthusiasts and nature photographers because it is home to a wide variety of flora and fauna. Numerous species, including Arabian leopards, gazelles, hyenas, foxes, and various bird species, can find habitat in the rugged terrain. The

Jebel Samhan Nature Reserve is a crucial area for conservation because of its population of critically endangered Arabian leopards.

- **Trekking:** For those who enjoy hiking and trekking, Jebel Samhan Nature Reserve provides excellent opportunities. The mountains and valleys are traversed by a number of paths and trails that let travellers explore the breathtaking scenery and find secret treasures along the way. Trekking through the reserve offers a close encounter with the natural world and the opportunity to see rare animals and plant species.

- **Opportunities for Photography**: Jebel Samhan Nature Reserve offers a wealth of photo opportunities due to its stunning landscapes and diverse wildlife. Take pictures of the wild cliffs' untamed beauty, the expansive mountain top views, and the fascinating wildlife in its natural settings.

- **Scenic Drives:** Travellers frequently choose to explore the nature reserve by car. The reserve's winding roads and picturesque drives provide expansive views of the mountains, valleys, and coastline. Keep an eye out for wildlife sightings as you travel through the reserve and pause at designated viewpoints to take in the breathtaking views.

- Jebel Samhan Nature Reserve offers the perfect setting for camping amidst the natural world. Create a campfire and spend the night outside in designated areas. You can experience the wonders of the celestial world while stargazing thanks to the reserve's clear and unpolluted skies.

- The region surrounding Jebel Samhan Nature Reserve is rich in history and culture, which has cultural significance. The Dhofar region's traditional arts and crafts can be found, as well as nearby traditional villages where you can explore and learn about the local way of life.

It's important to respect the environment when visiting Jebel Samhan Nature Reserve, adhere to any rules or guidelines that may be in place, and leave no trace of your trip. This will make it easier to maintain the remarkable reserve's biodiversity and natural beauty for future generations to enjoy.

Dhofar: Land of Frankincense

The southern Oman region of Dhofar, also referred to as the "Land of Frankincense," is well-known for its historical and cultural significance in relation to the production and trade of frankincense. What makes Dhofar such a captivating place is as follows:

- Sacra trees, which are also referred to as frankincense trees, are found in Dhofar. The priceless resin known as frankincense, which is produced by these trees and has long been highly prized. Visitors can see how the resin is extracted from the tree's bark by skilled locals using the traditional methods of frankincense harvesting.

- **Frankincense Souks and Markets:** Visiting Dhofar's bustling souks and markets is a must-do activity. These historical markets provide an intriguing look into the frankincense trade. Along with other regional goods like perfumes, incense burners, and traditional Omani handicrafts, you can buy different grades of frankincense.

- **Landscapes with Frankincense Trees**: The frankincense trees that dot the landscapes of Dhofar give the region a distinctive and fragrant atmosphere. These trees can be seen and smelled as you travel through the area, particularly in the Dhofar Mountains and Dhofar Desert. A captivating backdrop is provided by the frankincense tree-covered hills and valleys.

- **Frankincense Museum:** The Frankincense Museum provides a thorough understanding of the history, production, and significance of frankincense in the area. It is located in Salalah, the capital of Dhofar. The museum features artefacts, exhibits, and hands-on activities that explore the frankincense's ancient customs and rich cultural heritage.

- **Historical Sites:** There are many historical sites in Dhofar that are connected to the frankincense trade. The historic port city of Al Baleed, a UNESCO World Heritage Site, is one noteworthy location. Visit the Land of Frankincense Archaeological Park to learn more about the area's maritime and trading history and explore the ruins of a formerly bustling city.

- **Natural Beauty:** Dhofar offers more than just frankincense's historical legacy. The area is renowned for its breathtaking natural beauty, which includes verdant greenery, immaculate beaches, and majestic mountains. The Khareef, Salalah's monsoon season, turns the dry desert into a lush paradise that draws tourists with its cool weather and vibrant vegetation.

- **Festivals and Events:** Dhofar holds a number of festivals and events to honour the local history and culture. Traditional performances, music, visual arts, and cultural exhibitions are presented at the Salalah Tourism Festival, which takes place during the Khareef season. During these celebrations, guests can observe the vibrant traditions and customs of Dhofar.

A trip to Dhofar offers a singular chance to experience the rich heritage, gorgeous scenery, and fragrant traditions of the Land of Frankincense. Learn more about the cultural importance of frankincense in this alluring area of Oman by exploring the markets, museums, and natural wonders of the area.

Salalah:A tropical paradise

Salalah, a city in southern Oman's Dhofar region, is frequently referred to as a "Tropical Paradise" because of its exceptional climate and breathtaking natural beauty. Here are some things that make Salalah enticing:

- **Khareef Season:** From June to September, Salalah experiences a monsoon season known as the Khareef. The area experiences a remarkable transformation during this time, going from a desert to a lush green environment. The Khareef creates a picturesque and refreshing atmosphere by bringing cool temperatures, light rain, and a thick fog that covers the mountains.

- Rolling hills covered in greenery and waterfalls: Salalah experiences an explosion of vegetation during the Khareef season. Visitors can see colourful landscapes dotted with banana plantations, coconut groves, and lush palm groves. Ayn Athum and Ayn Khor are two stunning waterfalls in the area that add to the tropical atmosphere by cascading waters through rocky cliffs.

- Salalah is home to pristine beaches with soft white sand and crystal-clear turquoise waters. Visitors can unwind and enjoy the sunshine while swimming in the warm Arabian Sea. Al Mughsail Beach, with its dramatic cliffs and blowholes, and Al Fazayah Beach, renowned for its serenity and natural beauty, are two well-liked beaches.
- **Historical and cultural landmarks:** Salalah is home to a thriving past. The historic ruins of Al Baleed Archaeological Park, a UNESCO World Heritage Site, can be explored by visitors and offer insights

into the area's maritime and trading history. With its traditional architecture and bustling market stalls, the Al Husn Souq provides an opportunity to experience Omani culture while shopping for regional handicrafts, spices, and frankincense.

- The Qara Mountains are a stunning range known for its untamed beauty and picturesque vistas. They are close to Salalah. The surrounding valleys, canyons, and wadis can be seen in breathtaking detail from hikes or scenic drives through the mountains. The varied flora and fauna that inhabit the mountainous terrain make it a haven for photographers and nature enthusiasts.
- **Heritage of Frankincense:** Salalah, which is a part of the Dhofar region, has a long history with the frankincense trade. To learn more about the origins, manufacture, and

cultural significance of this priceless resin, visitors can explore the Frankincense Land Museum in Salalah. To buy frankincense and related goods, you can also go to traditional souks and markets.

- **Traditional Festivals**: During the monsoon season, Salalah hosts a number of exciting cultural festivals, including the Salalah Tourism Festival and the Khareef Festival. Visitors can immerse themselves in the local culture and traditions at these events, which feature traditional music, dance performances, crafts, and Omani food.

Salalah is a truly alluring location thanks to its tropical climate, lush surroundings, immaculate beaches, and rich cultural heritage. Salalah offers a distinctive fusion of natural beauty and Omani traditions that are sure to leave a lasting impression, whether you're looking for relaxation, adventure, or a cultural experience.

OUTDOOR ACTIVITIES

Scuba Diving and Snorkeling

The diverse marine ecosystems and underwater wonders can be explored through scuba diving and snorkelling in Oman. What makes snorkelling and scuba diving in Oman special is as follows:

- **Rich Marine Biodiversity:** Oman is home to a diverse range of marine life, making its coastal waters a haven for divers. In some seasons, you might see vibrant coral reefs, tropical fish, sea turtles, rays, dolphins, and even whale sharks.

- **Precious Dive Sites:** Along its coastline, Oman is home to a number of dive sites, each of which offers distinctive underwater environments and experiences. Divers and snorkelers of all skill levels can enjoy underwater pinnacles, coral gardens, and vibrant reefs.

- **Daymaniyat Islands:** The Daymaniyat Islands are a protected nature reserve off the coast of Muscat and are well known for their outstanding diving and snorkelling opportunities. These islands are home to abundant marine life, including reef sharks, turtles, and a wide variety of vibrant fish species, as well as pristine coral reefs.

- **Musandam Peninsula:** Located in northern Oman, the Musandam Peninsula is renowned for its breathtaking fjords and clear waters. In this region, diving or snorkelling offers the chance to see stunning cliffs and mountains in addition to the underwater scenery, which includes vibrant corals and a variety of marine species.

- **Daymaniyat Islands:** Another well-liked diving location in Oman is the Daymaniyat Islands, which are close to the city of Barka. With great visibility and a variety of marine life, these islands have been designated as a marine nature reserve. Divers and snorkelers can examine coral reefs, come across marine turtles, and see a variety of fish species.

- Ras Abu Dawood is a picturesque dive site in the Dhofar region of Oman that is well-known for its impressive coral formations and the chance of seeing dolphins and whale sharks. Divers and snorkelers love it because of the clear waters and a variety of marine life.

- **Professional Dive Centers**: Oman is home to well-known dive establishments that welcome divers and snorkelers of all skill levels. These facilities provide snorkelling trips, guided dives, and equipment rentals to make sure divers have a fun and safe time underwater.

The coastal waters of Oman offer a playground for exploration and discovery, whether you're an experienced diver or a novice snorkeler. Scuba diving and snorkelling adventures in Oman will allow you to fully immerse yourself in the underwater world, admire the magnificence of coral reefs, and come face to face with fascinating marine life.

Dolphin Watching

In Oman, dolphin watching is a well-liked and unforgettable activity that gives tourists the chance to see these graceful animals in their natural environment. Here are some things that make dolphin watching in Oman special:

- Dolphins are abundant in Oman's coastal waters, including the Indo-Pacific humpback dolphin, bottlenose dolphin, spinner dolphin, and Risso's dolphin species. There are many opportunities for sightings during dolphin watching excursions because these marine mammals are frequently observed in large pods.

- **Year-round Availability**: Dolphin watching is available all year long in Oman. However, the summer months, from April to October, are typically the calmest and warmest for dolphin sightings. The likelihood of seeing dolphins in greater numbers is higher during this time.

- **Scenic Boat Trips**: Dolphin watching excursions in Oman typically include a boat trip along the coastline, providing panoramic views of the Arabian Sea and the arid Omani landscape. Keep an eye out for dolphins as you sail through the water as they may swim alongside the boat, leap through the waves, or exhibit other acrobatic behaviours.

- Oman is committed to responsible dolphin watching practices that guarantee the animals' welfare and conservation. Local business owners follow regulations that maintain a secure distance from the dolphins in order to prevent any disruption of their normal behaviour. This strategy encourages eco-friendly travel and aids in the preservation of the marine ecosystem.

- Dolphin watching tours in Oman frequently include educational commentary from knowledgeable guides who share intriguing facts about dolphin behaviour, habitat, and conservation initiatives. You'll learn more about these intelligent beings and how crucial it is to protect their natural habitat.

- **Bonus Sightings:** Although dolphin watching is primarily focused on these magnificent mammals, you might also see other marine life while out on your adventure. A variety of seabird species, flying fish, and sea turtles can all add to your experience, so keep an eye out for them.

- **Photographic Opportunities:** Those who enjoy taking photos of dolphins in their natural habitat will find that dolphin watching offers fantastic chances to do so. You can record unforgettable memories of these lovely animals, from playful jumps and tail slaps to synchronised swimming.

It's crucial to pick reputable, licensed tour guides who put dolphin welfare first and adhere to responsible tourism guidelines when taking part in dolphin watching excursions. With their help, you can have a fascinating and moral experience seeing dolphins in their natural environment and helping to protect and conserve them.

Hiking and Trekking

Outdoor enthusiasts can explore Oman's varied landscapes by hiking and trekking there, from the country's untamed mountains and wadis to its coastal cliffs and desert dunes. What makes hiking and trekking in Oman thrilling is as follows:

- **Hajar Mountain Range:** With breathtaking vistas and strenuous trails, the Hajar Mountain Range is a well-known hiking destination in Oman. Jebel Shams, Oman's highest peak, offers an exhilarating trekking experience thanks to its imposing canyons and stunning surroundings.

- Jebel Akhdar, also referred to as the "Green Mountain," is renowned for its terraced agriculture, fruit orchards, and cool climate. Numerous hiking trails are available on the mountain, allowing visitors to fully appreciate the natural beauty of the mountains and take in the expansive views of the valleys and settlements below.

- **Wadis**: Oman is well known for its beautiful wadis (dry riverbeds), which are great for hiking and exploring. Popular options include Wadi Shab, Wadi Tiwi, and Wadi Bani Khalid because they provide chances to hike through constrained canyons, swim in clear pools, and find undiscovered waterfalls.

- **Coastal Trails**: The coastline of Oman is home to gorgeous cliffs, secret coves, and immaculate beaches. The coastal trails offer a distinctive hiking experience because they combine picturesque ocean views with untamed terrain. For coastal hikes, the Musandam Peninsula and the Ras Al Jinz Turtle Reserve are particularly well-liked.

- **Trekking through the desert**: Oman's deserts, like the Wahiba Sands, provide a special trekking opportunity amidst golden sand dunes. Trekking across the desert gives you the chance to take in how vast the area is, enjoy the hospitality of the Bedouin people, and spend nights under the starry desert sky.

- **Cultural Trails**: Numerous hiking trails that pass by historical sites and traditional villages showcase Oman's rich cultural heritage. Both the Al Jabal Al Akhdar and the Al Jebel Al Misht Treks offer chances to visit historic forts and villages and engage with the local populace.

- **Nature Reserves**: Oman is home to a number of protected areas, including the Dhofar Mountains and the Jebel Samhan Nature Reserve, which provide a range of ecologies and hiking trails. These reserves allow you to appreciate Oman's natural beauty and wildlife because they are home to distinctive flora and fauna.

Consider the weather, pack enough water and supplies, and make sure you have the right hiking equipment when organising a hiking or trekking adventure in Oman. For safety reasons and to learn more about the local environment and culture, it's also a good idea to hire local guides or sign up for pre-planned tours.

Oman's landscapes offer countless opportunities for memorable hiking and trekking experiences, regardless of whether you are an experienced hiker or a nature enthusiast looking for exploration.

Rock Climbing

Oman's diverse array of cliffs, mountains, and untamed landscapes make for an exciting experience for rock climbers. What makes rock climbing exciting in Oman is as follows:

- **Different Rock Formations**: Oman is blessed with a variety of different rock formations, such as sandstone, limestone, and granite. Climbers have a variety of options and challenges thanks to this diversity, which ranges from vertical walls and crags to intricate rock features and bouldering possibilities.

- **Magnificent Mountains:** Oman's mountainous terrain, including the Hajar Mountain Range and Jebel Akhdar, provides incredible opportunities for rock climbing. These enormous peaks offer a variety of trad, sport, and bouldering climbing options, with routes appropriate for climbers of all levels.

- **Jebel Misht:** For rock climbers, Jebel Misht, which is situated in the Jebel Akhdar region, is a well-liked vacation spot. It offers numerous routes, such as multi-pitch climbs, with breathtaking views of the nearby valleys and hamlets.

- **Wadi Bani Awf:** Wadi Bani Awf is another well-known rock climbing location in Oman and is situated in the Hajar Mountain Range. It has difficult limestone cliffs with routes that range in difficulty from moderate to advanced.

- **Cliffs along the coast:** Oman's dramatic coastline offers opportunities for rock climbing along the coast. With its rocky cliffs and fjords, the Musandam Peninsula provides a distinctive seaside climbing experience with breathtaking Arabian Sea views.

- **Professional Advice:** It is advised to hire local guides or sign up for climbing tours if you are new to rock climbing or are unfamiliar with the terrain in your area. In addition to ensuring your safety, knowledgeable guides can help you find the best climbing routes based on your preferences and skill level.

- The rock climbing community in Oman is expanding, and it has access to climbing facilities and well-kept climbing routes. This includes climbing gyms where climbers can train and hone their skills in Muscat and other major cities.

- It's crucial to have the right climbing supplies on hand before starting a rock climbing adventure in Oman, including harnesses, helmets, ropes, and suitable footwear. Always put safety first, evaluate the difficulty of the routes, and be mindful of local laws and climbing ethics.

Rock climbers of all skill levels can enjoy the varied rock formations, majestic mountains, and coastal cliffs of Oman. So Oman's captivating landscapes will offer an unforgettable rock climbing experience, whether you're a beginner looking for an introduction to the sport or an experienced climber seeking new challenges.

Watersports

For adventure seekers, Oman's coastal waters offer a wide variety of thrilling watersports activities. Here are some well-liked water activities you can engage in in Oman, from scuba diving in the Arabian Sea to jet skiing through the waves:

- **Scuba diving:** Investigate the thriving coral reefs and marine life of Oman's underwater environment. Scuba diving enthusiasts can experience breathtaking marine biodiversity and come in contact with colourful fish, turtles, rays, and other fascinating creatures thanks to the abundance of dive sites along the coastline, including the Daymaniyat Islands and the Musandam Peninsula.

- **Snorkelling**: Without extensive training, snorkelling is a great way to explore Oman's underwater treasures. Don your mask, snorkel, and fins, then plunge into the shoreline of Oman's crystal-clear waters. Discover coral reefs, swim with tropical fish, and get up close to the stunning marine ecosystem.

- **Jet Skiing:** Feel the rush as you soar across the waves on a powerful jet ski. Rent a jet ski from one of the many beachfront resorts or water sports facilities and experience the rush of adrenaline while cruising through the open water and feeling the wind in your hair.

- **Kayaking**: Use a kayak to explore the mangrove forests, fjords, and inlets along Oman's coastline. Gain a closer understanding of nature as you paddle through calm waters and admire stunning coastal scenery. A tranquil and environmentally friendly way to enjoy Oman's natural beauty is by kayaking.

- Try your hand at stand-up paddleboarding (SUP), a popular water sport that combines stability, core strength, and calmness. Take a relaxing boat ride along the calm waters, take in the coastal scenery, or even try SUP yoga.

- **Kitesurfing**: Oman's windy coastline makes for perfect kitesurfing conditions. Put your harness on, launch your kite, and use the wind's energy to ride the waves. Oman offers places like Masirah Island and Al Sawadi Beach for an exhilarating kitesurfing adventure, regardless of your level of experience.

- **Fishing**: Oman's coastal waters offer some of the best fishing in the world. For a day of deep-sea fishing, charter a boat and set sail. Test your fishing prowess while attempting to catch a variety of fish, such as tuna, dorado, and snapper.

- When taking part in watersports, it's crucial to put safety first. Make sure you have the required tools, adhere to safety precautions, and, if necessary, seek the right instruction from qualified instructors. While participating in watersports in Oman, remember to respect the environment and keep in mind the efforts being made to conserve the marine environment.

- The watersports scene in Oman offers activities for all tastes, whether you're looking for deep-sea exploration, fast-paced excitement, or a tranquil connection with nature. Dive in, ride the waves, and make lifelong memories along Oman's breathtaking coastline.

PRACTICAL TIPS FOR A SMOOTH TRIP

Local Etiquette and Customs

To show respect for the nation's culture and traditions, it is crucial to be aware of the local etiquette and customs when visiting Oman. To remember, bear the following in mind:

- Oman is a conservative nation, so modest attire is expected, especially in public spaces and places of worship. Clothing that covers the shoulders, knees, and cleavage is appropriate for both men and women to wear.

  Women might think about donning loose-fitting, leg- and arm-covering clothing. Women should also carry a headscarf in case they need to cover their hair in particular circumstances.

- Warm hospitality and politeness are two qualities that Omanis are renowned for. A handshake is customary when introducing oneself to the community, but men should wait for Omani women to do so.

  It is considerate to use salutations like "As-salaam alaikum" (peace be upon you). When addressing someone, it's also customary to use titles and honorifics like "Sayyid" (for men) and "Sayyida" (for women), followed by their full name.

- Omani culture places a high value on respect and modesty. Avoid showing affection in public, especially between couples, as it is improper. Respecting elders, religious leaders, and traditional practices is highly valued.

- When taking pictures of people, especially women, always get their consent first and respect their decision if they say no. It's important to be aware of local laws and customs because photography may be restricted or outright forbidden in some places or at specific events.

- **Ramadan**: Show respect for those who are fasting if you visit Oman during the holy month of Ramadan. When it's daylight, refrain from eating, drinking, or smoking in public. While it is not necessary for non-Muslims to fast, it is polite to avoid these activities in public out of respect for those who are fasting.

- The proper way to enter a mosque is to remove your shoes and dress modestly. Mosques are typically open to visitors who are not Muslims, but it is important to show respect and adhere to any instructions or rules that may be given.

- **Food customs**: The culture of the Omani people heavily depends on their cuisine. It is customary to accept an invitation to a meal in an Omani home and express gratitude for the food. Since the left hand is traditionally regarded as unclean, use your right hand when eating. Furthermore, it is considerate to sample a bit of everything that is offered.

- Alcohol consumption is not permitted in public places in Oman because of Islamic law. For non-Muslim visitors, alcohol is nevertheless accessible in hotels and restaurants with a licence.

You will not only demonstrate your appreciation for Omani culture by respecting and following local customs and etiquette, but you will also ensure a more pleasurable and peaceful visit.

Transportation in Oman

You have a variety of options for getting around Oman and taking in the sights when it comes to transportation. The primary forms of transportation in Oman are as follows:

- Travellers who want the independence and flexibility to explore Oman at their own pace frequently opt to rent a car. At airports and major cities, there are numerous national and local car rental agencies. Make sure your international driver's licence is up to date and that you are familiar with the local traffic laws.

- **Taxis:** In Oman, particularly in cities like Muscat, taxis are widely available. They are simple to locate at designated taxi stands or when you are on the street. Although Omani taxis are typically metered, it's a good idea to haggle or confirm the fare with the driver before the trip.

- **Public Buses:** Major cities and towns are connected by an extensive public bus network that runs throughout Oman. These buses are an inexpensive option for moving between and within cities, and they are operated by the Oman National Transport Company (Mwasalat). The Mwasalat website has bus routes and schedules.

- **Private Transfers:** For greater convenience, especially for larger groups or families, private transfers, such as hire cars or vans with drivers, can be arranged. With this choice, you get individualised service and can adjust your itinerary to suit your needs.

- **Domestic Flights:** There are domestic flights between major cities like Muscat, Salalah, and Sohar if you want to cover long distances quickly. The two primary airlines offering domestic flights within the nation are Oman Air and SalamAir.

- **Ferries**: Because Oman is a coastal country, there are ferry services that connect its ports. If you want to travel to the Musandam Peninsula or explore the coastal regions, this is especially helpful. Between places like Muscat, Khasab, and Shinas, ferries run frequently.

- **Off-Road Vehicles:** Off-road vehicles are a well-liked option for more daring tourists to explore Oman's rough terrain, particularly in areas like the desert or mountainous regions. It's crucial to possess the necessary expertise and understanding of off-road driving techniques, as well as the necessary licences, if necessary.

Think about things like the distances between destinations, the state of the roads, and your ideal level of comfort and flexibility when planning your transportation in Oman. In remote areas or during severe weather, it is advisable to check for any travel advisories or updates.

Accommodation Options

You can choose from a variety of lodging options in Oman to fit a variety of preferences and budgets. Oman has accommodations for every taste, whether you're looking for opulent resorts, cosy inns, or more affordable options. Consider some of the typical accommodations listed below:

- Oman has a wide selection of hotels and resorts that can accommodate guests with a range of tastes and financial constraints. In major cities like Muscat, Salalah, and Sohar, you'll find a wide range of options, from boutique hotels and beachfront resorts to globally renowned luxury chains.

  These accommodations provide cosy lodgings, and cutting-edge amenities, and frequently come with restaurants, spas, and swimming pools.

- **Desert Camps:** If you want to have a distinctive experience while visiting Oman's desert regions, think about staying at a desert camp. These camps offer traditional lodgings, typically in the form of tents or huts designed after Bedouins, allowing you to fully experience the desert setting.

  Many camps provide memorable desert experiences by providing activities like camel rides, dune-bashing, and stargazing.

- **Guesthouses and Inns:** In some parts of Oman, guesthouses and inns are an affordable and authentic lodging option. These more intimate settings and opportunities to mingle with locals are provided by these smaller businesses. They might offer fundamental comforts and a more authentic Omani experience.

- Serviced apartments are a good choice for people looking for longer stays or more self-catering lodgings. These apartments are suitable for families or travellers who prefer the convenience of cooking their meals because they frequently come fully furnished and furnished with a kitchenette or full kitchen.

- **Eco-Lodges and Retreats:** Oman's dedication to sustainability and natural beauty has sparked the growth of eco-lodges and retreats. The eco-friendly and fully outdoor experience that these accommodations emphasise is key. They are frequently situated in picturesque areas, like mountainous or coastal regions, enabling visitors to re-establish a connection with the natural world.

- **Traditional Omani Homes**: In some regions of Oman, you might be able to book a stay in a traditional Omani home that has been turned into a hotel. These homes typically have local furnishings and traditional architecture, giving visitors a genuine sense of Omani culture and heritage.

When choosing a place to stay, keep things like location, accessibility to activities or attractions, amenities, and price in mind. It's a good idea to make reservations in advance, especially during busy travel times or for well-known locations.

You can choose from a variety of lodging options to make your stay in Oman comfortable and memorable, whether you're looking for luxury, peace, or a closer connection with Omani culture.

Language and Communication

Arabic is Oman's official language, and a large portion of the local populace speaks it. English is also widely spoken and understood, especially in urban areas, popular tourist destinations, and among those who work in the tourism sector. Here are some details regarding communication and language in Oman:

- **Arabic:** Learning a few fundamental greetings and phrases in Arabic can be useful while travelling in Oman. This demonstrates respect for the community's culture and can improve how you interact with Omani people. "As-salaam alaikum" (peace be upon you) is a typical Arabic salutation, as is "Shukran" (thank you) to express gratitude.

- English is widely spoken and understood, especially in tourist destinations and businesses like hotels, restaurants, and retail stores. Many Omani people, especially the younger generation and those employed in the tourism industry, speak English fluently. For the majority of your needs, like getting help, ordering food, or asking for directions, it's usually simple to communicate in English.

- **Tourist Guides:** Hiring a local tour guide can be helpful if you prefer more individualised assistance. These tour guides can enhance your travel experience by giving you in-depth knowledge about the landmarks, history, and culture of Oman. They frequently speak English fluently.

- **Information and Signage:** The majority of Oman's signage, including street signs, government announcements, and schedules for public transportation, is displayed in both Arabic and English. Visitors will find it simpler to navigate and comprehend the most crucial information as a result.

- **Mobile Internet and Translation Apps:** When travelling in Oman, think about using a mobile internet connection to improve communication. This will give you access to language learning resources or translation apps that can help with simple conversations or translations as needed.

- **Non-Verbal Communication:** Non-verbal cues like gestures can also be used to convey information. It's important to be aware that in Oman or Arab culture, specific gestures or body language may have different meanings than in other parts of the world. You can avoid any unintentional misunderstandings by showing respect and adhering to local customs and norms.

Overall, since English is widely spoken and understood in Oman, language shouldn't be a significant obstacle when travelling there. The ability to communicate effectively and improve your travel experience in Oman, however, can be attained by making an effort to learn a few simple Arabic phrases and exhibiting respect for the nation's language and culture.

Recommended Travel App

Several helpful travel apps can improve your experience and make your trip to Oman more convenient. Here are a few suggested travel applications for Oman:

- The official Oman tourism app, Visit Oman, offers detailed information on the nation's sights, lodging options, dining establishments, and events. Additionally, it provides travel guides, itineraries, and interactive maps.

- **Oman Air:** If you're flying with Oman Air, you can manage your reservations, check-in online, monitor the status of your flight, and access other practical features like airport guides and special deals through their official app.

- The Oman National Transport Company (Mwasalat) offers information on public bus routes, schedules, prices, and real-time bus tracking through this app. You can use it to navigate Oman's public transportation and plan your routes.

- **Google Maps:** Google Maps is a trusted and well-liked application for getting around and learning about new places. It offers thorough maps, instructions, and information on interesting locations. For use when you don't have an internet connection, it is also possible to download offline maps of Oman.

- You can browse nearby restaurants, read reviews, and order food for delivery or takeout using Zomato or Talabat, two well-known food delivery services in Oman. They can discover restaurants and sample regional food.

- You can quickly convert currencies and check exchange rates with the help of the dependable currency converter app XE Currency. When comparing prices and working with Omani Rials (OMR), this can be useful.

- **Oman Post**: The Oman Post app enables you to track shipments, find post offices, and access other postal services if you intend to send or receive mail or packages during your trip.

- Staying in touch with locals, tour guides, or other travellers can be accomplished using WhatsApp or Viber, two widely used messaging services. They make it simple and affordable to communicate by providing free online voice, video, and messaging services.

- To ensure easy access, remember to download these apps as well as any necessary offline maps or content before your trip, especially if you might not have reliable internet connectivity.

Even though these apps can be useful, it's always a good idea to have a backup plan or carry printed maps and important contact information just in case anything goes wrong with the technology.

APPENDIX

Useful Phrases in Arabic

Here are a few practical Arabic expressions for visitors to Oman:

Greetings:
- Hello: Marhaba
- Good morning: Sabah al-khair
- Good afternoon: Masaa' al-khair
- Good evening: Masa' al-khair
- How are you?: Kaif halak? (to a male) / Kayf halik? (to a female)
- I'm fine, thank you: Ana bekhair, shukran

Basic Expressions:
- Yes: Na'am
- No: La
- Please: Min fadlak (to a male) / Min fadlik (to a female)
- Thank you: Shukran
- You're welcome: Afwan

- Excuse me: 'Afwan
- I'm sorry: Asif

Directions and Transportation:
- Where is...?: Ayna...?
- How much is this?: Kam hadha?
- Where is the bus station?: Ayna mahattat al-autobus?
- Can you help me?: Mumkin mosa adati?
- I would like a taxi, please: Oreedu taxi, min fadlak (to a male) / min fadlik (to a female)
- Stop here, please: Qif hunak, min fadlak (to a male) / min fadlik (to a female)

Ordering Food and Drinks:
- I would like...: Ooredoo...
- Water: Ma'
- Coffee: Qahwa
- Tea: Shay
- Breakfast: Al-iftar
- Lunch: Al-ghada

- Dinner: Al-'asha

Asking for Help:
- I need help: Ahtaju musaada
- Can you speak English?: Hal tatakallam al-ingliziya?
- I don't understand: La afham

Numbers:
- One: Wahid
- Two: Ithnayn
- Three: Thalatha
- Four: Arba'a
- Five: Khamsa
- Ten: Ashara
- Twenty: Ishrun
- Hundred: Mi'a
- Thousand: Alf

During your visit to Oman, these words and phrases should come in handy for basic interactions. Keep in mind that most Omani people are amiable and appreciate any effort made to speak their language.

Emergency Contacts

The following emergency numbers should be remembered when visiting Oman:

- The phone number for emergency services (police, fire, ambulance)
- Call the Royal Oman Police (ROP) at 9999.
- +968 2450 8000 Sultan Qaboos Hospital in Muscat
- Ambulance Emergency Medical Services: 1444
- 9999 traffic accidents
- +968 2456 5555 Coast Guard
- Hotline for the Ministry of Tourism: +968 2412 9140
- The emergency number for Oman Airports Management Company (OAMC): +968 2435 5888

It is recommended that you store these phone numbers in your phone or keep them nearby in case of an emergency. Upon arrival, it's also a good idea to enquire at your place of lodging or nearby tourist information centres about specific emergency contact numbers and procedures.

CONCLUSION

In conclusion, the "Travel Guide to Oman 2023" offers a thorough resource for tourists looking to discover Oman's undiscovered attractions. This guide covers a variety of topics related to travelling in Oman, such as useful information, visa requirements, health and safety advice, the best time to visit, and issues relating to money and currency.

The Sultan Qaboos Grand Mosque, the Royal Opera House Muscat, the Mutrah Souq, the Bait Al Zubair Museum, and the Qasr Al Alam Royal Palace are just a few of the highlights of the Muscat capital city that are highlighted in this article.

The guide goes into more detail about Oman's natural wonders, including its breathtaking beaches, Ras Al Jinz Turtle Reserve, Wahiba Sands, Wadi Bani Khalid, and the picturesque coastal drive from Muscat to Salalah. The majestic mountains of Jebel Shams, Jebel Akhdar, the Nizwa, and Jebel Al Misht are also explored, providing opportunities for trekkers, hikers, and rock climbers.

The guide also emphasises Oman's diverse cultural heritage, which includes Bedouin tradition, traditional arts and crafts, and UNESCO World Heritage Sites like Bahla. It goes into detail about the extraordinary adventures of desert camping, going to Al Rustaq's hot springs, and touring old forts.

The guide offers insights into Omani cuisine and traditional treats for foodies, and it covers natural attractions like Wadi Shab, Bimmah Sinkhole, and Jebel Samhan Nature Reserve for nature lovers. Additionally, the guide highlights the historical importance of locations like Dhofar, Salalah, and Sohar.

The guide emphasises local etiquette and customs, transportation options, lodging options, language, and communication advice, in addition to providing useful information. An appendix with additional resources and information is also included, along with suggestions for useful travel apps.

Visitors to Oman will be able to fully immerse themselves in the beauty, culture, and adventure that the nation has to offer with the help of this travel guide. Oman is a location that guarantees a distinctive and unforgettable experience, whether travellers are looking to unwind on the stunning beaches, discover ancient ruins, or go hiking through the mountains.

Fond Farewell

We wish you a warm farewell as your journey through the "Travel Guide to Oman 2023" comes to an end. We hope that this guide has given you insightful knowledge, practical information, and inspiration for your Oman adventure.

I hope your travels are full of breathtaking scenery, fascinating cultural encounters, and lasting relationships. May each step you take bring you nearer to the heart and soul of Oman, whether you choose to wander through the historic forts, swim in the glistening waters, or hike the majestic mountains.

Take with you the warmth and friendliness of the Omani people, the sounds of traditional music, the tastes of regional cuisine, and the lifelong memories as you depart.

Have a safe trip, and may Oman's natural beauty and your discoveries along the way bring you joy and discovery. Goodbye and may your next adventure be right around the corner until we meet again.

Made in the USA
Columbia, SC
07 February 2024

31598129R00128